INTERDIMENSIONAL
UNIVERSE

ABOUT THE AUTHOR

Philip Imbrogno has researched UFOs and other paranormal phenomena for over thirty years and is recognized as an authority in the field. A science educator at the secondary and collegiate levels for twenty-eight years, he has been interviewed by the *New York Times* and *Coast to Coast AM*, has appeared on NBC's *Today Show* and *The Oprah Winfrey Show*, and has been featured in documentaries on the History Channel, A&E, Lifetime, and HBO. Imbrogno worked closely with many top UFO investigators, including Dr. J. Allen Hynek and Budd Hopkins. He can be contacted by e-mail at Bel1313@ yahoo.com.

INTERDIMENSIONAL
UNIVERSE

THE NEW SCIENCE OF UFOS,
PARANORMAL PHENOMENA
& OTHERDIMENSIONAL BEINGS

PHILIP IMBROGNO

Llewellyn Publications
Woodbury, Minnesota

First Edition
Second Printing, 2009

Cover design by Kevin R. Brown
Interior book design by Joanna Willis
Interior photos courtesy of the author

SPACE (Search Project for Aspects of Close Encounters) is a support system for close-encounter witnesses and is engaged in a proactive re-search program. It is based in New York City, active since March 1992. Harold Egeln is the founder and director.

Llewellyn is a registered trademark of Llewellyn Worldwide, Ltd.

Library of Congress Cataloging-in-Publication Data
Imbrogno, Philip J.
  Interdimensional universe : the new science of ufos, paranormal phe-nomena & otherdimensional beings / Philip Imbrogno.—1st ed.
      p. cm.
  Includes bibliographical references and index.
  ISBN 978-0-7387-1347-2 (alk. paper)
  1. Human-alien encounters. 2. Unidentified flying objects—Sightings and encounters. 3. Parapsychology. I. Title.
  BF2050.I45 2008
  001.942—dc22
                                                                        2008016028

Llewellyn Publications
A Division of Llewellyn Worldwide, Ltd.
2143 Wooddale Drive, Dept. 978-0-7387-1347-2
Woodbury, MN 55125-2989, U.S.A.
www.llewellyn.com

Printed in the United States of America

To the giants and pioneers of paranormal research
who showed me where to look for answers
by allowing me to stand on their shoulders.

ALSO BY PHILIP IMBROGNO

Night Siege: The Hudson Valley UFO Sightings

Contact of the 5th Kind

Celtic Mysteries in New England

CONTENTS

PREFACE

The most unforgivable sin in science is for scientists to claim that something exists when in fact they know that it does not. This is also true when researchers falsify or try to interpret information to suit their own personal beliefs and needs. It is also a travesty of science to say that something does not exist, especially when the scientists have not determined if in fact it does or does not. This is a persisting problem that we as paranormal researchers have had over the years with the study of the UFO phenomenon. Mainstream science has turned a deaf ear to the credible reports of encounters with something truly incredible. On the other hand, some UFO researchers also have been guilty of exaggerating the experiences of UFO witnesses and stretching the proof to prove the reality of the phenomenon. These researchers have also had predetermined ideas about what the UFO experience represents, and they have often manipulated the evidence to support and defend their own ideas. Science is the pursuit to understand the unknown, and if a scientist is going to be an objective researcher, then all egos must be put aside and only the evidence must be analyzed. Those who investigate UFO reports must begin their investigation with an open mind and collect only the facts. However, no matter how skeptical you are about UFOs, there are three things that can not be denied: UFO reports exist, they persist, and it's a global phenomenon.

I have been investigating and researching paranormal phenomena (which includes UFOs) for thirty years and must make it very clear that I investigate UFO reports and not UFOs themselves. This is why the study of UFOs can be so fleeting—we can only gather data on the effects the UFOs had on the environment and individuals. We are also limited to video, digital, and photographic images, which are not really good evidence, since most UFO evidence of this type is easily faked and still highly controversial. There are real images out there of these mysterious objects, but each year it is getting more difficult to determine what is authentic and what is not. It is my personal belief that there are a number of different types of intelligent beings responsible for the overall UFO experience. The UFO experience includes sightings, channeling, abductions, and other forms of contact. I myself have had four sightings and know that it is all very real, and we need to know more about the true nature and purpose of this intelligence. In this book, I have proposed new ideas to help shed some light on this age-old phenomenon. I have written the book so that both the beginner and the more experienced investigator will benefit from the information and research gathered from my thirty-plus years in the field. The chapters that cover some of the most famous UFO cases in history should not be overlooked by well-read UFOlogists, since they contain new and important information that has never been published.

My previous books, *Night Siege*, *Contact of the 5th Kind*, and *Celtic Mysteries in New England*, all document my work in the area of paranormal research. This book is the last book I will write that focuses on the UFO situation. This is because unless I personally make contact, I have gone as far as anyone can go by gathering information in the field. To get a better understanding of my work and how it evolved over the years, I would suggest that you read my previous works before you read this one.

To me, the past thirty years of research in the field has been more of an adventure and a spiritual journey of awareness than a scientific project. During my long journey, I have met a great number of interesting people and was privileged to work with some of the top researchers in the field. These people included Dr. J. Allen Hynek, John G. Fuller, Budd Hopkins, John Keel, John Burton, and Whitley Strieber, and I also give special thanks to the publishers of *UFO Magazine*, Nancy and Bill Birnes, for educating the public and keeping them informed and updated concerning the current UFO situation. I hope this book gives you the motivation to continue the research that I and many others have started, because if we are ever to solve the UFO mystery, we must have a clear view of what we left behind and what lies ahead. We can only accomplish this by standing on the shoulders of those who came before us.

Philip J. Imbrogno
August 2007

ONE

ROSWELL: THE STORY THAT WILL NOT FADE AWAY

It has been more than six decades since the beginning of what has been called the "modern" UFO era, and although the phenomenon seems to come and go in cycles, there is no indication that sightings and close encounters have vanished to become part of our mythology. It all began on June 25, 1947, when Kenneth Arnold (fig. 1), a private pilot, witnessed a number of unknown objects flying over the Cascade Mountains in Washington State at great speed. When he was asked by the media to describe what the strange aerial objects looked like, he replied, "They looked like saucers skipping across water." Thus the term "flying saucer" was born to describe the unknown aircraft that Arnold saw that day. The truth of the matter is, Arnold never said that they were saucer- or disk-shaped—he was trying to describe to the press how the objects moved across the sky. When he drew the unknown aircraft

Figure 1. Kenneth Arnold describing what he saw in 1947.

he witnessed for federal investigators, his artistic representation showed the mystery object as looking like a boomerang or chevron and not a saucer. However, they were still called flying saucers by the media, and from that time until today, the citizens of planet Earth have reported seeing thousands of them each year to the government leaders of the world, who have just turned their backs on the reports as if they did not exist.

Because of the great magnitude of sightings, the matter was turned over to the Air Force, where several project studies were carried out from 1951 to 1969 to determine if the mysterious objects were a threat to national security. Many UFO researchers whom I have talked with over the years now think that these projects, which had the names Sign, Grudge, and Blue Book, were nothing more than a public-relations front by the government to make people think that the reports of UFOs were being taken seriously, when in fact many were not. During that time, the Air Force was indeed interested in UFO reports, but only those that were sighted over or near military bases or other secured areas. The Air Force and other government agencies treated many of the people who had witnessed something truly incredible as crazy or claimed they were pathological liars looking for publicity. The negative effect of this attitude was that those people who had UFO encounters were afraid to report them because they were afraid that they might be labeled as nuts. Recently, due to the efforts of a civilian group called Citizens Against UFO Secrecy (CAUS), who obtained official government documents using the Freedom of Information Act (FOIA), it became clear that many of the civilian reports were taken seriously by the intelligence organizations of this country. The documents proved that the governments of the major powers of planet Earth were very concerned about the sightings of flying saucers and what they might possibly represent.

ALIENS BECOME PART OF OUR CULTURE

Today there is a renewed interest in UFOs, aliens, life on other planets, and extraterrestrial contact. The twenty-first century has marked a new era of discovery for the human race with the exploration of the surface of planet Mars and the launch of the New Horizons spacecraft to Pluto. According to the International Astronomical Union, during the past thirteen years over two hundred planets outside our solar system have been discovered circling stars within our sun's galactic neighborhood. This is an indication that the galaxy might be teeming with life, and perhaps contains many technological civilizations.

The movies in our local theaters and on television are filled with stories of alien contact and, through this same media, images of extraterrestrials and UFOs are being used by many businesses to help sell their products. Most people today now embrace the idea that we are not alone in the universe and many expect first contact within their lifetime. The idea for the movie *Men in Black (MIB)* did not come from an imaginative Hollywood screenwriter—it was taken from actual reports of witnesses who were visited by mysterious men after a close encounter. Although the elusive MIBs claim to be government agents, no agency will acknowledge that they exist. Their message to the witnesses of a UFO is always the same: be silent or face the consequence.

So why is there still such a great interest in UFOs after all these years? The answer may lie in the fact that the governments of the world may have had actual contact with a race of aliens for several decades and are slowly trying to introduce the idea into our culture. Although no one, including myself, has proof that this has actually taken place, it could explain why images of the "gray" alien beings with the large heads and eyes can be found on pencils, lunch boxes, television, and in video games and the movies. They are becoming quite familiar figures to the next generation of the twenty-first century, a generation that may be undergoing programming to accept them without fear. Also, millions of people around the world continue to report encounters with an alien intelligence, and many claim to have made contact with the pilots of the UFOs. These incidents are too numerous to ignore, and they can no longer be denied. Is there any hard evidence that we have been visited by an extraterrestrial intelligence in modern times? UFO researchers feel the strongest evidence for this comes from an alleged crash and recovery of an extraterrestrial spacecraft just outside Roswell, New Mexico, by the United States government in 1947.

During the first week of July 1997, I received a call from a TV producer who told me that she was planning to do a program on UFOs that was to be aired in the fall. As the conversation continued, she said that she was very surprised to reach me since she thought I would surely be at Roswell for the fiftieth anniversary of the "UFO crash." I told her that I really didn't see the point in going, because what took place there happened fifty years ago and there would be nothing new to discover since the trail is now cold. The Roswell incident has always been somewhat of an enigma to me. Did a spaceship from another world really crash in the desert of New Mexico? Most people who have read about the Roswell crash do not know that the object that was allegedly recovered was not a disk, but delta in shape. Because it did happen so long ago (by human standards), and because most of the people who were around at that time have passed away or were too young to remember, it's difficult to find out what really took place. Also, when a story is told over and over again for many years, it has a tendency to become more fantastic and detailed than the original version.

Since it is not the purpose of this book to rehash the Roswell case, I will not get into the finer details of the alleged Roswell, New Mexico, UFO crash. I do feel it is important to cover the basic information for those who know little or nothing of one of the most famous (or infamous) UFO incidents of modern times. You must be very careful about what you read about the Roswell incident, because over the years it has developed almost a cult following all over the world, and much of the information contained in many publications both printed and electronic has very little to do with the real facts. During the mid-1980s, I was fortunate enough to obtain the original news stories from a number of papers including the *New York Times* and the *San Francisco Chronicle*. After reading these first accounts of what took place at Roswell, it was quite clear how greatly recent television presentations and books on the Roswell incident deviated from the original 1947 stories. The following is a synopsis of the Roswell incident, based on information from the 1947 news stories and my own investigation, and from the files of the late Dr. J. Allen Hynek, files that were given to me several months after his death in 1986.

THE ROSWELL INCIDENT

On July 7, 1947, Mr. Mac Brazel, a rancher who lived seventy-five miles northwest of Roswell, New Mexico, contacted the local police authorities and reported that he found a great deal of metallic-looking debris on the ranch that he worked near the town of Corona, New Mexico. For those of you who were not born during the late forties and early to mid-fifties, it was a time of the beginning of a great wave of UFO sightings in the United States. It was also just a couple of years after World War II, so everyone was quite paranoid about the Russians, and the people of our country (USA) had total trust in our government. Mr. Brazel told police that he thought that the debris might be part of a flying saucer and that it should be investigated. The sheriff of the police department then contacted Roswell Army Airfield, which in turn sent Major Jesse Marcel and two officers to investigate. Their job was to look at the debris to see if it was unusual and, if so, bring it back to the base for further evaluation. Major Marcel arrived at the scene and thought that the material was strange, so he collected what he could and brought it to Roswell Airfield that same evening.

A short time later (perhaps the next day), a public information officer for the base released a statement to the press that the Army Air Force had recovered the remains of a flying saucer. General Ramey of the Eighth Air Force then ordered the debris flown to Fort Worth, Texas, for his personal inspection. When General Ramey looked at the debris, he and his staff recognized parts that to them looked like a weather balloon. He then turned over the material to the base scientists who identified the debris as the pieces of a balloon made of a new material that the Army was experimenting with (some say it was Mylar, the shiny material used in birthday balloons today). General Ramey then called a press conference to show reporters the debris, and he allowed them to photograph the materials found. Ramey told the press it was nothing more than a balloon and declared that the entire story of a crashed flying saucer was a misunderstanding.

This is not the end of the story. In the months and years that followed, doctors, nurses, military and civilian personnel who worked at the base, and people who lived in the area swear that a flying disk was recovered, as well as the bodies of a number of alien pilots. There are also claims by some Roswell residents that individuals were being silenced by government agents and that there was a growing conspiracy by the Air Force to hide the truth from the public about what really took place that day at Corona and Roswell.

DR. J. ALLEN HYNEK
AND THE ROSWELL CONNECTION

When I think of Roswell and the "crash" at Corona, I will always remember something the late Dr. Hynek told me back in 1984. He said, "It's not a question whether UFOs exist or not—they do—but are the reports made by people accurate? One problem that we have as researchers in this area is wondering if the witness is relating the story exactly the way it happened." Dr. Hynek did not imply that people were fabricating stories about UFOs; it's just that in many cases, witnesses to a UFO sighting, or any other paranormal event for that matter, have an unconscious way of adding detail to the story by filling in missing data to make it more comfortable for them to deal with and understand. In my thirty-plus years of collecting reports and interviewing people, I have found this statement made by Allen Hynek to be very true. This is why it is very important to have two or more witnesses to a paranormal event; as Dr. Hynek also once told me, "one witness is no witness." Since I will be mentioning

Figure 2. Dr. J. Allen Hynek.

Dr. Hynek in this book from time to time and will be quoting him on a number of his ideas about the UFO phenomenon, I would like to tell readers who are new to the UFO experience who this great man was and explain his contributions to science and UFOlogy.

Allen Hynek (fig. 2) was born on May 1, 1910, when Comet Halley was visible in the sky. In 1931, Dr. Hynek received a Bachelor of Science degree from the University of Chicago. In 1935, he was awarded a PhD in astrophysics from the university, where he worked and studied the evolution of stars at Yerkes Observatory. During World War II, Allen Hynek was a scientist at the Johns Hopkins Applied Physics Laboratory, where he helped develop the proximity fuse for the nuclear bomb, something that he regretted for the rest of his life. This is because Allen Hynek was a spiritual man and one of peace. In the years that I knew him, Dr. Hynek never had anything negative to say about anyone, even when his character was attacked by the UFO skeptics. When World War II was over, he returned to the Department of Physics and Astronomy at Ohio State University, rising to the position of full professor in only a few years. He was also one of the scientists who worked on the Apollo 11 moon mission, helping NASA select the first lunar landing site.

In 1951, in response to the overwhelming reports of un-identified flying objects, the United States Air Force estab-lished Project Blue Book and asked Allen Hynek to be their scientific advisor. When he began this job with the Air Force, he was very skeptical of UFO reports and thought they were just a fad that would eventually go away. However, after years of investigating hundreds of reports and talking to count-less credible witnesses, his attitude changed. When Project Blue Book ended in 1969, Hynek started the Center for UFO Studies, which was the first civilian scientific clearing-house for UFO reports.

Allen Hynek was without a doubt the world's foremost authority on the UFO phenomenon, so when he told me he was skeptical of the Roswell "crash," I listened to what he had to say. Before we go on, I must mention that this was Allen Hynek's opinion concerning Roswell and at no time did he ever personally investigate the alleged crash himself. Dr. Hynek passed over on April 27, 1986, when Comet Hal-ley once again appeared in the sky. He was seventy-five years old. Years before his death, he often told me that he came into this world with the comet and would leave with it when it swung around the sun again, and this is exactly what hap-pened. Like Mark Twain before him, Allen Hynek came and went with Comet Halley.

When I questioned Dr. J. Allen Hynek about the Roswell incident and asked him if he thought that the crash was a real event, he replied that he felt that the entire story was a "fairy tale" that got out of hand and more exaggerated every time the story was told. When I asked him if he was sure of this, he replied, "Don't you think that I would have heard something about this since I was the scientific consultant to Project Blue Book for over twenty years? Don't you think I would have at least seen fragments of documents or would have heard rumors or got information from the many people that I knew in the intelligence organizations?" Dr. Hynek told me that he was sure that the so-called Roswell UFO crash was nothing more than an experimental new type of surveillance balloon that was classified as top secret at the time. He closed the subject by saying, "Roswell is like an old sore that keeps on popping up over the years and won't go away." He then refused to discuss the incident with me any further.

Did he know more than what he was telling? To this day I still ask myself that question. It may be that as open as Allen Hynek tried to be about the UFO phenomenon, even he may have been silenced on some matters. I do know that on a number of occasions Dr. Hynek was denied information about military encounters with UFOs, despite the fact that he was their "scientific advisor"; perhaps he really did not know much about the Roswell incident after all. Dr. Hynek told me about this top-secret balloon project in 1984; however, the project was not declassified until 1995, when it was released to the people of this country on nationwide television as an attempt by the Air Force to put the Roswell incident to rest for all time. Needless to say, when the information was released, it caught my attention.

PROJECT MOGUL

When the Air Force released its documents on Project MO-GUL, the top-secret project that they believed was responsible for the Roswell incident, I was all ears and glued to the TV. This was a time before I had the Internet, so my only quick resource for getting up-to-date information was from CNN. Speaking of CNN, I know for a fact that the network was told to carry UFO stories and was one of the only stations at the time that did so. One of the reasons was that in the eighties and early nineties, Ted Turner had (and I think still has) a great interest in UFOs. He had read my earlier book *Night Siege: The Hudson Valley UFO Sightings* and was so fascinated by it that he had sent reporters to New York to cover the sightings. One of the reporters told me that not only were they collecting information for a number of future CNN newscasts about the UFO sightings in the Hudson Valley, but they were reporting directly to Ted Turner and turning the information over to him.

The televised CNN Roswell-MOGUL report was made by an Air Force public relations officer, 1st Lt. James Mc-Andrew, who held up in front of the TV camera a very thick book, which had the title, *The Roswell Report: Fact Versus Fiction in the New Mexico Desert*. I thought it was strange that the government would spend so much time just to publish a detailed report on an incident that they claimed never took place. During my six-year service with military intelligence, I knew that this was a tactic that they used when they wanted to cover up the real truth. As Lt. McAndrew began to talk about Project MOGUL, I turned on my VCR and began to listen closely to not only every word he said, but also how he said them. I also watched his facial expressions and other body movements as he talked, since from my past experience with the military I knew a few tricks on how to read people's body language while they talked to tell what is really on their minds.

Project MOGUL was the idea of Dr. Maurice Ewing of Columbia University. He had conducted research during the war and found it was possible to hear explosions underwater thousands of miles away using a new microphone developed by the Woods Oceanographic Institution. Dr. Ewing thought that if sound waves from explosions could be picked up over long distances in the ocean, then this idea might also apply to the air. The only problem was that water is a great deal thicker than the atmosphere, and any high-school student knows that sound waves travel faster and maintain their intensity when moving through a medium that is dense, so the microphone device would have to be very sensitive. This idea was important to the government, because in 1947 there were no spy planes or surveillance satellites to monitor the Russians. This was a practical way to listen in on the world to see if anyone was testing a nuclear bomb. In order for the device to work, it had to be placed very high in the atmosphere, so a new technology had to be developed. This project was called MOGUL, and from 1947 until the mid-nineties, it remained classified as top secret. We do know that several large balloons were tested around the United States, but the majority of them were flown out of Alamogordo, New Mexico, between May 28 and June 7, 1947. This would place the last launch well before the Roswell incident. By early 1948, the Air Force began to have serious doubts on how effective Project MOGUL was, and shortly after this time, the project was terminated.

When Lt. McAndrew was asked about the "alien bodies," he replied that on a number of occasions, dummies were sent up with the balloons and dropped to test pilot ejection devices and protective gear. He told reporters that the so-called alien bodies may have been the dummies used in this experiment. I found this all a little strange—it seemed to me that the Air Force went through a great deal of trouble to explain away a UFO incident that they considered a "closed file" a very long time ago. I watched my video copy of the presentation several times, and it is my opinion that Lt. McAndrew was not telling the entire truth, that he was simply relating a cover story written by his superiors.

After remembering what Dr. Hynek told me and then hearing the report about Project MOGUL, I decided to put the Roswell incident to rest for a while, at least in my own mind. However, that was to change a few months later when I was introduced to an extraordinary person who identified himself as one of the engineers who was taken to Roswell to examine debris at the alleged crash site. The individual in question was a retired electrical engineer with top-secret security clearance. He was one of the top electronic experts in the country, and during World War II he was often called to look at captured German technology involving electronic guidance systems. I have no reason to doubt the story that he told me, but on the other hand there is no evidence to fully accept that what took place is a true recollection of his experience. His name was John, and I promised not to release his story until after his death. You see, John was ill with cancer and his doctors gave him between one and two years to live. John passed away in 1993, and the following is a transcript of his story as told to me in the summer of 1992. This story was never published, and I kept it in my files until the right time. I feel it is an important part of this book and although many well-known UFO investigators have criticized me in the past for withholding information (such as the 1984 UFO encounter over the Indian Point, New York, nuclear reactor), I waited until the right opportunity presented itself for John's story to be published. The following is a transcript of what he told me a few months before his death.

JOHN'S STORY

"Sometime during the first week of July 1947, just before sunrise, I was called on the telephone and was told to get ready to do some work for the government. This was not unusual since I was often called at a moment's notice and would have to travel all around the world to look at new technology that was captured by the Allies. This became more frequent, especially after the end of the war, so what was then taking place was not uncommon, and I expected to be taken to some remote military base to inspect a new electronic gadget that no one was able to figure out.

"I was living in New York City at the time, and a car was sent to pick me up and take me to the airport. Usually the guy who would be sent to get me would be in a military uniform, most of the time Army, but this fellow was in civilian clothes and dressed in a dark blue or black suit. I really did not think too much of his clothes at the time, I just thought it was somewhat strange, so I asked for his identification. His ID said that he was a Colonel Roberts of military intelligence. The rest of his papers looked in order, so I didn't ask any more questions. Although he was dressed in civilian clothes, he really didn't act like one; he acted like a typical G-man. That's what we used to call them back in the old days, those men who worked for the intelligence organizations. We went to the airport and I got on a military plane, and there were three others on the plane. The G-man also boarded the plane and sat next to us and asked if we would please not engage in conversation with him or each other, since all questions would be answered on a need-to-know basis only.

"It was daybreak now, and I could tell we were heading west. After four hours of flight, we landed on an airstrip. I didn't know where it was at the time, only from the terrain that it was somewhere in the southwest United States. Later I found out that we landed on an isolated landing field just several miles from Roswell Air Base in New Mexico. As I got out of the plane I noticed that there were three buses, and I could see other technical experts that I had worked with in the past in line ready to board the vehicles. There were also two other planes on the runway, but parked to the side with their engines running. The strange thing was that all the aircraft, except for the one I was on, were painted a flat black with no markings on them. I do not know what time it was since we were asked to remove our watches before we got on the plane. I think it was late morning, of course I was judging this by the time of the year and the angle of the sun in the sky above the eastern horizon. The ground was damp and the air was hot and humid as if there had been a very bad storm recently. The buses that we boarded were also unmarked and the windows were blacked out. It was obvious that whoever was in charge of this operation wanted to keep their identity secret and us in the dark.

"I was told to enter the first bus and that it was ready to go, since they were awaiting the arrival of our plane. The driver was once again a G-man dressed in civilian clothes, and I found out that all fourteen of us on the bus were engineers of some standing. Some I even knew personally. I thought that perhaps the other buses also contained experts but from different scientific fields. Later I was to find out that this was the case, but now you have to realize that in these three buses were the top people that the government used for technical and scientific consultation. For all of us to be here like this, I knew that something big was brewing, something that was bigger than postwar jitters.

"After traveling a half-hour or so—I totally lost track of time—the bus came to a stop and the driver opened up the door and told us that we had arrived at our destination. I walked out of the bus and saw five tents with two guards with weapons, wearing Army uniforms, in front of each opening. There were also many Army vehicles in the area, and I would say fifty or seventy-five people in military uniform, which all looked like Army. We were divided into groups and then directed to a tent. It seemed to me that this was postwar related and they were only going to allow us to see what we had to. The tents were divided into sections that contained something for our particular expertise. I did see one person who I worked with closely in the past being directed to the far-end tent. He was a biomedical researcher, and I wondered why he was there unless they had tissue samples or bodies of something that was once living.

"I was directed to the second tent and asked to enter and examine its contents. I saw piles of debris in sections on the floor, and what I saw made me realize that this was something our government did not have, or any other government of the world for that matter. There were pieces of metal that had a dull silver appearance to them, and when I picked up the larger pieces, I was surprised to find they had no weight at all. It was as if I had nothing in my hand—I couldn't even feel it resting on my skin. I had to grab it with both hands and squeeze it to make sure it wasn't some type of illusion. Some of the pieces were very thick and they looked like they weighed a ton, but they were lighter than a feather. Inside the tent we had a great number of tools and instruments at our disposal and were told to use whatever we wanted. They made us work in teams and allowed us to discuss our findings, but they said everything would be recorded. The metal would not bend or crush, even with more than three thousand pounds of pressure, and it would not react to a metal detector. I was taken to a closed-off cubicle in the tent and shown something that looked like the remains of a smashed control panel. Attached to the panel was something that I didn't recognize at the time, and I had no idea what the components were. I say this because years later I realized that what I saw was in fact something very similar to our computer chips of today. These, however, had a number of red crystals linked in their circuits, which were faintly glowing. There was also a device about the size of a cigarette pack, which had a pulsing red light on top of it. The electronic components once again were something that I was not familiar with at the time, but these components that I saw are now used in our computer technology of today. The device seemed to be giving off a signal, almost like an emergency distress beacon, but to whom? I modified an available receiver and found out it was transmitting on the 5-gigahertz band, a frequency that is used today, but unheard of at that time. The transmitter had no antenna, and I was shocked to see that it was extremely directional. To me this meant that someone was trying to mark their position before they crashed in this object, which I knew now were parts of some type of aircraft.

"We were allowed to examine the material for several hours and then were taken one by one into another tent, which I called the command tent, where we were debriefed. I was told that what I saw was a matter of the highest national security, and if information leaked out to the press, I could face a very stiff prison term. You have to remember that back in those days we trusted the government of the United States, since it was just after World War II and people did not question anything because they thought it was for the good of the country. I had to write a detailed report of my impression and analysis of the material and the components that I was allowed to examine. I never saw what I wrote in a report or document of any kind since it was taken away as soon as I finished. Usually when a transcript was completed, I was allowed to see the final document and check for errors before it became a permanent record, but not in this case. I wondered who these people were and why they had so much power. I am not intimidated easily, but these guys were very serious, had powerful backing, and were scary. I was taken back to New York and was never called again about this incident. What is even stranger, several weeks later I was paid in cash by a special military courier. At the time I really didn't know what I was seeing, but later realized that I saw the remains of parts of an aircraft that was not from this Earth. I am sure I was taken to see some of the components of an alien spacecraft that crashed near Roswell. What else could it have been?"

The conversation ended at that point, and I could not reach this person for several months. A close friend of his informed me that he had passed away shortly after he told me his story, a story he kept silent for over fifty years. However, at the time I took what was told to me as just another story about Roswell. This person really had no proof, just his word, but his experience made me consider the possibility that in 1947 an alien spacecraft did crash somewhere close to Roswell, New Mexico. At no time did this person ever see any alien bodies or an entire ship. He did see several dozen pieces that looked like the smashed remains of a technologically advanced aircraft of some type, a guidance system, and some pieces of metal that could have been the hull or another part of a supporting structure. I have no reason to doubt this claim, since the person reporting it had nothing to gain for telling me about the incident and this was the first time he mentioned the story to anyone since that day in 1947. Perhaps because he was dying, John wanted to get the story out and chose me to tell it to since he had read my book *Night Siege*.

John's story intensified my interest in Roswell, and during the autumn of 1992, I received a letter from a retired military man who had more to add about the United States government's involvement with UFOs. He gave me permission to publish the letter, provided that I not use his name.

AN INTERESTING LETTER

Mr. Imbrogno,

Today I received a wonderful Father's Day gift from my daughter. It was your book, *Contact of the 5th Kind*. She told me that it was the most informative book on UFOs and extraterrestrial contacts that she ever read. Knowing that I was a believer, it was the perfect gift for me and I was delighted. But before I had the chance to read it, I remembered an incident that I personally witnessed some fifty-one years ago. I then decided to tell you my story before I read the book so that I would not be influenced by anything I read. So here is my true story of events that I can recall to the best of my knowledge.

Everyone has heard of the Roswell UFO incident in 1947, but another incident happened at Roswell almost one year later in June or July 1948. I have never read anything about this, nor will hardly anyone acknowledge the happening. In February 1948, I was assigned

to the 509th Bomb Group at Walker Air Force Base outside Roswell, New Mexico. During one clear night in
June or July, I was the CQ [charge of quarters] in the
Group Headquarters building, next to the office of the
base commander, who was Colonel William Blanchard.
I was on duty that night, answering the phone and making a mail run into Roswell. Normally, it's a boring tour
of duty. However, that night at about 10 p.m., I received
a phone call from someone at the flight operations office. Something was happening at the edge of the flight
line; guards were reporting strange lights with no explanation. I got into my jeep and drove over to the operations area. A lot of people were standing around,
looking at the far end of the runway. I joined them and
this is what I saw to the best of my knowledge.

At the edge of the runway facing the desert, I saw
possibly a dozen round white lights in a horizontal formation hovering just off the ground. They were bright,
individual lights just hovering there. Then all of a sudden they shot up into the dark sky, going in all directions, then out of sight. There was no sound at all,
and everyone was baffled at this strange appearance.
I wrote the incident in my report, which was required
at the end of my duty shift, and forgot about it. The
next morning I learned that the base was placed on a
heightened state of emergency during the night. When
I tried to find out more information about the incident,
I was told nothing happened and that I should not talk
about it. This was very strange indeed.

The following day I noticed several high-ranking officers at our headquarters, and security was heightened around the base. I never found out what happened, except several people from Roswell reported strange lights in the sky that night also. Shortly after that I was discharged and returned home to Chicago. I re-enlisted in the Air Force, and in 1960 I was assigned to Fort Douglas, Utah. Rumors were flying that evidence of the 1947 Roswell incident was stored in a warehouse there. I located the building and it was guarded and listed as *secret*. Shortly thereafter, I was reassigned to Wright-Patterson Air Force Base in Ohio. There I learned from rumors that the evidence of the 1947 Roswell incident was stored in one of their warehouses. There again, the building was secured with numerous guards.

Could all of these events be a coincidence? When you group them all together, it appears that our government was hiding something. Could the stories of Roswell have real merit? It's been many years, but I can vividly recall what I had seen. I retired from the United States Air Force in 1969 as a senior master sergeant, and I consider myself open-minded. I do believe that something happened at Roswell in 1947 and again in 1948. I am looking forward to reading your book. Thank you for your time.

(Name withheld by author)

UFO SIEGE

Have there been any more recoveries of alien crashed vehicles since then? The answer to this question is that we may never know since they would be covered up. I have heard stories, from different parts of the world, of crashed and recovered alien ships, but the researchers who brought forth the information just don't seem to have enough details to make the stories sound convincing. I have also heard stories from ex-military people who think that Roswell was just a smoke screen for something else that happened close by involving actual face-to-face government contact with an alien intelligence. It was rumored that at least two of these alien crafts crashed near New Paltz, New York, and the other on an isolated section of Long Island in the late 1980s. The evidence for these alleged alien crashes was very weak, and in my opinion they are most likely the result of the overactive imaginations of zealous local UFO investigators.

According to reports made to government and civilian agencies, UFO sightings have escalated considerably around the world since the Kenneth Arnold sighting and the Roswell incident. If these objects are nuts-and-bolts vehicles, then it is logical to assume that there might be an occasional crash. From 1980 to 1990, people in the Hudson Valley area of New York reported seeing a giant UFO in the skies at a low altitude. A similar series of sightings then took place during the late eighties and early nineties in Belgium (Europe). All of the reports indicate that it was a large object, very dark in color, and triangular or boomerang in shape. On March 13, 1997, hundreds of people reported an enormous object in the night sky over Paulden, Arizona. The UFO was once again a triangle or boomerang and very similar to the object reported earlier in New York and Belgium. All the witnesses were consistent—they reported an object that appeared very huge and solid. But was it really? In all of these case studies, the people who witnessed the giant UFO tried to report the sighting to the authorities, but their words fell on deaf ears.

Although the Air Force claims no interest in UFO reports, they nevertheless take them very seriously. Less than fifteen minutes after residents in Arizona called Luke Air Base (which is more than one hundred miles south of Paulden, Arizona), witnesses reported seeing flights of F-16s in the area where the UFO was being seen. As the fighters approached the UFO, the object shot straight up and disappeared into the night sky. The sightings in Paulden, Arizona, were very dramatic indeed and, like the sightings in Belgium and New York, were witnessed by hundreds of people. Despite the multitude of reports from very credible witnesses, the authorities tried to convince the people that they saw nothing and that there were no UFOs.

To this day, the UFO phenomenon continues to be seen by millions of people around the world. From the evidence of just the reports, there is no doubt that there is an alien presence here on Earth. The worldwide reports of encounters are too numerous to simply ignore, yet the government and military of this country would have us think that the reports are just figments of our imagination. Just recently I did a radio talk show from Danbury, Connecticut, about UFOs. When I started talking about the government cover-up, I received a call from a flag-waving all-American who was very angry with me, stating, "There is no cover-up, and even if there was, the government does everything for our own good and we should not question anything that they do." It is this mentality that has given certain members of the government almost unlimited power, a power so great that they do not have to report their activities to Congress or even the president.

The new information that came to me concerning Roswell and the recent sightings around the world once again intensified my interest in the UFO phenomenon and inspired me to take a new, fresh approach and research the early days of UFO investigation by the United States Military. This was not an easy task since it required a great number of Freedom of Information Act requests and two visits to the National Archive in Washington DC.

TWO

IN THE BEGINNING

After the June 25, 1947, Arnold UFO sighting, the military and other government agencies of the United States were bombarded by reports of "flying saucers," so many reports that the military started to become concerned. People reported everything from "flying hubcaps," "flying dimes," "flying tear drops," and "flying ice cream cones" to "flying pie plates." However, what really seemed to concern them were the reports of the flying objects that were chevron in shape. The government also considered that mass UFO reports could be used to tie up communication channels, allowing for a secret Russian attack on the United States. To all my younger readers, although this might sound like paranoia today, this was the time of the start of the "cold war," and to Americans it wasn't a question of *if* the Russians would attack, but *when*. So it seems that the military initially considered that the flying saucer reports could have been a Russian ploy to clog up the communication channels just before a sneak attack.

PROJECT SAUCER╱SIGN

Shortly after the Arnold sighting, in response to the reports of "flying saucers," the government of the United States set up Project Saucer (also called Project Sign) as a clearing-house to look into some of the more verifiable reports. One can understand why the project was called "Saucer," since the objects came to be known as flying saucers; however, Sign was also used, since a few military people of high rank were looking for a sign as to what the UFOs actually represented. Project Saucer investigated three hundred domestic and thirty foreign cases of unidentified flying objects. The exact findings and statistics of both of these early government UFO investigations can be found by obtaining the documents from the Air Material Command and the National Archives. Because the documents regarding Sign and Saucer are now declassified, you should not have any trouble getting a copy mailed to you. I personally have my own documents and although there is a modest copy fee, by filing as a researcher you can get the fee waived. I was able to obtain copies at no cost simply by filing as a professional educator and author.

With the resources of the military, and a number of selected scientists and specialists at their disposal, Project Saucer (Sign) was able to explain over 30 percent of these sightings as being misinterpretations of stars, planets, weather balloons, aircraft lights, birds, optical illusions, and practical jokes. Project Saucer's evaluation team's final report was that there was no conclusive evidence that unidentified flying objects are real aircraft of unknown or conventional configurations. The report assured the public that there was no cause for alarm. According to a document obtained using the Freedom of Information Act by a number of researchers (including myself), Project Saucer was instructed to turn over all sightings of boomerang, chevron, or V-shaped objects to Army Intelligence for further evaluation (FOIA Document 1948-276548: Project Sign Conclusions). The reason why this branch of military intelligence ignored all reports except for the UFOs with the shapes mentioned above was not known until the 1990s, when a number of documents that were once classified as top secret were declassified and finally released to the American public and made available to researchers. I must stop to give credit to attorney Peter Gersten, and the authors of the book *Clear Intent,* Larry Fawcett and Barry Greenwood, who for over ten years filed numerous lawsuits against the military and intelligence organizations. Their legal actions resulted in obtaining hundreds of documents that involved the military and their secret interest in flying saucers. If it was not for the efforts of these three researchers trying to seek the truth, today we would still be in the dark in terms of what we know of the UFO-government connection. The following information comes from declassified documents that I obtained, which were once labeled as top secret by the Air Material Command, then a division of the Army Air Corps.

Figure 3. The Horten Wing: Could it have
been mistaken for UFOs in the late 1940s?

THE HORTEN FLYING WING

At the end of World War II, when the Allies entered Berlin
and other major cities of Germany, military officers were told
to search for German scientists and bring them to the United
States. One of these scientists captured was Wernher Von
Braun, the developer of the V-1 and V-2 rockets that caused
so much damage to England. Von Braun was found innocent
of war crimes and placed in charge of the American rocket
development program. The Army officers were also told to
search bunkers and secret bases for new technology that the
Nazis were rumored to have been developing. At that time,
military intelligence knew that Germany had developed the
jet fighter; however, it was put into use too late in the war
and was not of much use when Berlin fell to the Americans

and Russians. The searching American soldiers discovered a secret warehouse, and in it they found designs for a delta-shaped aircraft called the Horten Wing (fig. 3). There was evidence that the craft had been built, but the hangars were empty and only vague blueprints were found detailing the aircraft and giving very little technical information. It was feared that the Russians got there first and took the aircraft; this was of great concern to the military, since this new technology could give the Russians an edge in the struggle for power that was developing between the two countries.

HISTORY OF THE HORTEN WING

In 1930, two German brothers, Reimar and Walter Horten, had designed an all-wing aircraft with no vertical control surfaces of any kind. They began experimenting with the new design and carried out their first test in July of 1933 at the Bonn-Hangelar airfield. The very first flight was such a great success that the German government granted the brothers unlimited resources to finish their work. In 1940, the Horten brothers told Adolf Hitler that they were very close to finishing an aircraft that had a jet engine capable of speeds and altitudes greater than man had ever seen before. We do know that BMW (yes, the same company that makes the car) designed the engines; however, today the people who run the company in Germany have no record of this, since all documents from the end of the war were taken by the Soviet Union (Russians).

The documents and designs that were found in the hangar indicated that there were at least fifteen versions of this new type of aircraft. The later models had a range of 3,000 miles and could achieve a speed of 725 miles per hour, which is something that was considered impossible for that day. Furthermore, the craft itself was made out of a new material that would be invisible on radar; this new material seemed to be a high-impact plastic like Lucite or Teflon. The craft was also very light and could maneuver easily, and in combat it could outperform any aircraft that was available at the time. The high-ranking officers in Army Intelligence became very concerned because if the Russians did get to the hangar before the Americans and took the prototypes of this aircraft, it could mean a very serious threat to the security of England, the United States, and the rest of the free world. So when Ken Arnold spotted his chevron-shaped objects in Washington in 1947, the military and the newly formed intelligence agencies went on alert. What Arnold described was exactly what was in the diagrams found in the hangars in Germany. It was only two years after the war, but the top brass in Army Intelligence feared that this could have been enough time for the Russians to develop, build, test, and fly this aircraft. Army Intelligence speculated that a squadron of Russian Horten Wings may have flown in from Siberia, along Alaska, and into the United States as a test to see if they could get away with it. The military knew that the Horten Wing would be a hard object to pick up on radar because of its stealth design and because many of its components did not reflect radio waves. This meant that the aircraft would be practically invisible to any type of electronic surveillance.

When UFO reports started popping up all over the country, the United States Military decided to look into the sightings, but they kept a low profile and used the "flying saucer" story to make it look ridiculous so that the public would not take it seriously. In the late forties and early fifties when the sightings were of epidemic proportions, some people came forward with stories of being taken to Venus and Mars. These stories got quite a bit of attention by the media, and they made a once-worried public laugh at the sightings of UFOs or flying saucers. This was an advantage to the military, since they wanted to play down the idea that the "saucers" were real.

According to the documents, well into 1948 the American military was still quite concerned that the sightings of many flying saucers might be the Russian version of the Horten Wing flying over our country, and since there was already so much paranoia about the Russians during this time, they did not want to start a cold-war panic. By the end of 1949, after considerable investigation and hundreds of intelligence reports, the American military found out that the Russians were also having sightings of the same mysterious aircraft over their country. The military came to the conclusion that they were not Russian, since the Soviet Union seemed to be very concerned about the sightings and actually blamed the Americans or England for violating their air space with a new type of aircraft captured from Germany.

What really happened to the Horten Wing is not known, but it's interesting to note that our stealth fighters and bombers of today seem to be based on that design. There is a story that Nazi Germany recovered an alien ship in the African desert and used that technology to improve the Horten Wing, and that high-ranking pilots of the Luftwaffe took the craft to South America where they started a secret society, which still exists today. Of course this is just speculation from a number of unofficial sources, but nevertheless it's an interesting idea to think about.

The United States government then decided to look elsewhere for the cause of the UFO sightings.

PROJECT GRUDGE

Despite the military's attempt to discredit the sightings of UFOs, the reports kept on coming in at an alarming rate. The intelligence organizations and the military could not deny that there were unexplained reports, but according to the documents I obtained using the FOIA, no one knew what to do with them . . . the bottom line was that in many of the cases, credible people were reporting something truly incredible. The military then decided to continue investigating sightings of flying saucers, but thought that the name for the project—"Saucer" or "Sign"—might encourage people to report any light in the sky, since the media now identified the term flying saucer with extraterrestrial spacecraft. The only other problem was that no branch of the military wanted to take responsibility for investigating the UFO sightings, so they kept on passing the new reports around to the different branches of the military like a hot potato. Congress was not satisfied with the way the reports were handled, so they gave the job of looking into the sightings to the newly formed Air Force. This decision was most likely made because the UFOs or flying saucers were up in the sky and Congress thought that it was the Air Force's responsibility.

Project Grudge replaced Project Saucer/Sign in 1949. The name was selected by the commanding officer of the Air Technical Command, since they now had the burden of dealing with the thousands of reports each year. So to them, the name "Grudge" expressed how the Air Force felt about processing and investigating the UFO reports made by civilians.

At about the same time, the commander of the Air Force ordered the activation of Air Force Regulation 200-2, which instructed all military personnel (especially pilots) to report a UFO sighting directly to their commanding officer. Failure to comply with this order was an Article 15 (commander's punishment) or a court martial. It was clear that the Air Force did not want sightings of UFOs made by soldiers and airmen to get into the hands of the media before they were debriefed. While I was in the military (1969–74), I looked up AFR 200-2, and it was still in effect and being strictly enforced. I thought it was strange that this regulation should still be on the books when the Air Force publicly stated that UFOs did not exist.

Project Grudge took the investigation of UFOs into the Dark Ages. The interviewing of witnesses was more like the Spanish Inquisition than a scientific investigation. The public as well as Congress were still not satisfied with the way UFO reports were handled, so Project Grudge did not last very long. By August of 1949, it issued its last and only report, with detailed comments by Dr. Hynek, who at this time was a part-time scientific consultant for the Air Force. The following information and conclusions are directly from the Project Grudge documents that I was able to obtain using the Freedom of Information Act. Since the documents are now declassified and in the public domain, the details of the report can now be published. Out of 244 sightings that Grudge investigated, only about 75 remained unidentified. The Grudge report recommended that investigations into the UFO sightings should stop because of the following reasons:

1. The number of sightings across the country has slowed down and the number of reports continues to decline each month. This indicates that the flying saucer craze is dying down.

2. Sightings of anomalies aerial objects should only be investigated if they clearly indicate and have realistic technical applications, or if the sighting takes place near or in a secure area or military base.

3. Most reports were in fact misinterpretations of conventional aircraft, stars, planets, or even hoaxes. The numbers of unidentified reports are such because of insufficient data.

4. It is recommended that the data for this project be declassified and made available to the American public to educate them about the sightings.

On December 27, 1949, the Air Force issued a press release that Project Grudge was closed and that the Air Force was no longer interested in collecting and investigating UFO reports. Despite an Air Force statement telling the American people to please not call them if they see a flying saucer, the reports continued, and by 1950 they again increased considerably in number.

WHAT ABOUT THE FBI?

One would think that if there were a threat to the security of the United States, the FBI would be involved, but their part in UFO investigation at this time was minimal. Reports and other information about "flying saucers" was kept away from the eyes of FBI director J. Edgar Hoover by Air Intelligence, and, because of this, the FBI set up its own investigation team, not only to investigate and collect UFO reports, but also all types of paranormal phenomena. The television show *The X-Files* was based on documents that the FBI at one time was investigating unusual phenomena. Although the project was not called the X-Files, the reports and investigations were sent to a location called the X Archives. This is where the producers and the writers for the hit show may have gotten the title.

The following information was taken from a document classified as secret and then declassified. The document was later obtained through the Freedom of Information Act in 1980 by a number of researchers, including myself, and copies of it are always on display at UFO conventions across the country. This was an internal FBI memo that was exchanged between two assistant directors to Director J. Edgar Hoover. It was dated not long after the Kenneth Arnold sighting and the Roswell incident.

"Air Intelligence advised of another creditable and unexplainable sighting of flying saucers. Air Intelligence still feels flying saucers are optical illusions or atmospherical phenomena, but some Military officials are seriously considering the possibility of interplanetary ships.

"You will recall that Air Intelligence has previously kept the Bureau advised regarding developments pertaining to Air Intelligence research on the flying saucer problem. Air Intelligence has previously advised that all research pertaining to this problem is handled by the Air Technical Intelligence Center located at Wright-Patterson Air Force Base, Dayton, Ohio; that approximately 90 per cent of the reported sightings of flying saucers can be discounted as products of the imagination and as explainable objects such as weather balloons, etc., but that a small percentage of extremely creditable sightings have been unexplainable.

"Colonel C. M. Young, Executive Officer to Major General John A. Samford, Director of Intelligence, Air Force, advised on October 23, 1952, that another recent extremely creditable sighting had been reported to Air Intelligence. A Navy photographer, while traveling across the United States in his own car, saw a number of objects in the sky which appeared to be flying saucers. He took approximately thirty-five feet of motion picture film of these objects. He voluntarily submitted the film to Air Intelligence who had it studied by the Air Technical Intelligence Center. Experts at the Air Technical Intelligence Center have advised that, after careful study, there were as many as twelve to sixteen flying objects recorded on this film; that the possibility of the objects being weather balloons, clouds or other explainable objects has been completely ruled out; and that they are at a complete loss to explain this most recent creditable sighting. The Air Technical Intelligence Center experts pointed out that they could not be optical illusions inasmuch as optical illusions could not be recorded on film."

The document then goes on to say that Air Intelligence would like the FBI to forward them flying saucer sightings since they knew that many of the reports were being denied to them. This document ends with a hand-written comment from J. Edgar Hoover, which states:

"I would do it but before agreeing to it we must insist upon full access to discs [flying saucers, UFOs] recovered. For instance in the [illegible] case the Army grabbed it and would not let us have it for cursory examination." (Hoover may have been referring to the Roswell crash and recovery.)

The 1948 memo in script was confirmed by the FBI as being the handwriting of J. Edgar Hoover. Once again, this part of the document can be obtained by the FOIA and has been put on display by a number of civilian UFO organizations and clubs.

So it appears that from a very early time the agencies were working against each other and each was collecting information secretly about the flying saucers for their own research and purposes. Because of this competition, a conflict developed between the CIA, Army Intelligence, Naval Intelligence, and NASA—a conflict that placed the American public in the middle, denying them the truth about the UFO situation.

ENTER PROJECT BLUE BOOK

Just eight months after Project Grudge closed down, the team listed the bulk of their cases as explained. Some of the explanations involved light reflections and mirages that were so complex that an alien spacecraft would have been easier to believe. The Air Force hoped that the reports would stop, but they did not; if anything, they intensified.

In March of 1952, Grudge II went public as an attempt to analyze the UFO reports from a scientific and psychological point of view. The question that scientists assigned to the project asked was, "Why are people seeing and continue to report strange lights in the sky if they don't exist?" Grudge II then changed its name and went public as Project Blue Book, and for the next seventeen years it remained the official UFO research program of the United States. It is rumored that the reason why the project was called "Blue Book" was because the data was stored in blue folders and notebooks. Also, Blue Book sounded a little less invasive than Sign, Saucer, Grudge, or Grudge II. The staff of Blue Book was only a handful of people, and they had a small office at Wright-Patterson AFB. To make things look official, Dr. Hynek was brought on as a full-time scientific consultant. He later told me that he accepted the position because nobody else wanted it, no other scientists of his standing were bold enough have their names associated with UFOs. At this point, the study of the UFO phenomenon was considered taboo by the scientific community. Allen Hynek was their scientific consultant, yet he personally told me that he was denied information regarding UFO sightings around secret military bases.

Blue Book's mission was much different than its predecessors' because its role in investigations was determined by the CIA. The exact date that the CIA got involved with UFOs is not clear, but from that time until today they seemed very interested in collecting reports. Blue Book ended in 1969 and determined that the UFO phenomenon did not represent a threat to the security of the United States and there was no scientific value in the reports. Allen Hynek later admitted that Blue Book was nothing more than a public relations front to satisfy the people of the United States and that the unexplained reports were sent to the CIA for further investigation. Later in his life, just before he passed over, Allen Hynek had this to say about Project Blue Book:

"All the years I was associated with Project Blue Book showed that the project did not exhibit any scientific interest in the UFO phenomenon. Such lack of interest in my opinion belies any claims of a government cover-up; they just didn't care. Turnover in the Blue Book office was high, and sooner or later the officer in charge would be sent out either by promotion or retirement. If you look at the project from an objective point of view, it would appear that Blue Book was not a front, but a foul-up, but serious reports were channeled to the CIA and Naval Intelligence."

Allen Hynek himself went from being a skeptic to accepting that UFOs were real. Dr. Hynek was quoted many times as saying, "I was told to explain these things away, but how long could I go on by telling these people that they saw nothing or they were crazy? So I decided to start my own personal research" (quote from Allen Hynek when he appeared on *Good Morning America* in 1984). When Blue Book closed down in 1969, Dr. Hynek went on to study UFOs on his own and started the Center for UFO Studies, which was to be a scientific clearing-house for reports. Later in his life, Dr. Hynek actually had a sighting himself, something that he very rarely talked about, so this also convinced him of the reality of the UFO experience.

NO LONGER IN THE
FLYING—SAUCER BUSINESS

By 1969, the government and military claimed that they were no longer in the "flying-saucer business," but documents obtained after 1969 show that the CIA, Naval Intelligence, and the FBI were still collecting UFO reports. Although with the help of the Freedom of Information Act (which is now overruled by the Patriot Act), UFO researchers were able to obtain hundreds of once-classified documents. However, for reasons of "national security," most of these documents were censored, making them just about useless. Once again, when it came to UFOs, the only thing that the government let the American public see was what they wanted us to see. It was also discovered that over one hundred of these documents were held and not turned over to the public because of (once again) national security. In response to this, the civilian organization Citizens Against UFO Secrecy (CAUS) took the agencies known to have UFO documents (primarily the CIA) to court. Without even seeing the documents, the judge ruled that the public had the right to access them, and he ordered the CIA to turn them over to civilian research organizations. The attorney for the CIA then protested and asked the judge to meet with him in his chamber room. When the judge returned a short time later, he reversed his decision and said that the public does not have the right to know the information that is contained in the documents because they do fall under the National Security Act. Once again, UFO researchers were left empty-handed, and all they had was a stack of documents that were partially blacked out. Since 9/11, it has become very difficult to obtain information from any government agency about UFOs or any other topic because of the Patriot Act. The Patriot Act, which was meant to "protect" us from terrorism, has also taken away some of our rights as American citizens and given more power to the military.

THREE

THE MODERN ERA

In response to the military and government agencies literally botching up the investigation of the UFO phenomenon by not releasing information to the public, a number of private-civilian UFO organizations began to spring up. These organizations included the National Investigations Committee on Aerial Phenomena (NICAP), the Aerial Phenomena Research Organization (APRO), the Center for UFO Studies (CUFOS), and finally the Mutual UFO Network (MUFON). There were also about a hundred smaller groups that all appeared during the same time frame, but many of them just fizzled out and NICAP, APRO, CUFOS, and MUFON remained the largest and most dominant organizations.

These organizations and clubs appeared because UFOs made it big in the American media and were a popular topic in the movies. There were TV shows, magazines, feature films, books, and gatherings of witnesses and researchers in what were later to be called UFO symposiums and conventions. I can remember a number of popular "shock" talk shows on television in the sixties whose most popular subject involved not only people who had UFO sightings, but also individuals who claimed to have been abducted by aliens or taken for a ride in a "spaceship" to Venus, Mars, or a nearby star system. Most of these people who had these extraordinary claims were ridiculed by the host and the audience. I must admit that the stories were very laughable, and later I wondered if some of these people were actually government plants with the purpose of making the UFO phenomenon look so ridiculous that no one would believe it or report a sighting for fear of being called crazy. Whatever the reason was, these fantastic stories or claims of being taken for a ride in a flying saucer or having sex with aliens took away the credibility that was needed to do a serious study of the UFO experience. As the years passed, the publicity seekers and hoaxers seemed to vanish as if being drawn into a black hole after having their fifteen minutes of fame, but the UFO sightings continued.

MY EARLY YEARS

In the early to mid-sixties I had a great interest in astronomy, and the idea of UFOs being some type of spacecraft from another star system visiting our tiny planet out in the galactic boondocks for exploration and scientific purposes fascinated me. I began reading every book that I could get my hands on and made sure to watch all the television talk shows and newscasts about the phenomenon. I followed the work of the early pioneers in this field who wrote the first books about what were still called "flying saucers," which by the way sold very well at that time; they included John

Keel, John Fuller, and Frank Edwards. The theme of most of these books was that UFOs were extraterrestrial spaceships visiting this planet for scientific purposes. Quite a few of these early books are still available today and considered classics in UFO literature.

There was one writer/researcher at the time who emerged with a theory about the UFOs that was so controversial that even the true believers rejected his ideas at the time. I consider this person a true pioneer in the field of paranormal research, a person who I believe set the foundation for an understanding of the true nature of the UFO phenomenon. This researcher's name is John Keel (of *The Mothman Prophecies* fame), and his idea was that UFOs may not be spaceships, but something more exotic, something perhaps not from our universe but another dimension or parallel reality. Keel's work was criticized by many researchers and writers in the 1960s through the '80s, and Allen Hynek was considered to be one of his greatest critics. I had the pleasure of working with and talking to John Keel on a number of occasions, and I found him to be a man of extraordinary insight, intelligence, and talent. Later, before his passing, Dr. Hynek told me that he thought that John Keel was correct and right on target about the true nature of the UFOs. When I told John this, he was very surprised, since for decades he and Dr. Hynek never agreed on anything.

In order to fully understand the direction in which I am heading with this book, it is important that my readers have an understanding how the UFO phenomenon evolved in our society and our minds. The classic cases must be covered because they are very important to a study of UFOs. Although many of these classic encounters have been presented in the past with prejudice by UFO investigators who I feel swayed the evidence to make the cases look like visitations of alien beings in spacecrafts, I will present each case with just the facts. However, they nevertheless provided a path to our current understanding of the UFO experience. Although seasoned researchers may know a great deal about the UFO cases presented in this chapter, the material should be read and not skipped over since I have added new information from the Allen Hynek files and my own investigation.

THE CLOSE ENCOUNTER OF FATHER GILL

Over the years, Dr. Hynek and I discussed a number of extraordinary UFO sightings he investigated, some of which were before my time as a UFO investigator. One of the cases that he was most impressed with took place in 1959 in Papua, New Guinea. He related to me the case details of a missionary priest by the name of Father William Booth Gill. Hynek told me that this was one of the cases that was the "straw that broke the camel's back" and made him accept the reality of the UFO phenomenon.

On April 5, 1959, sometime in the late evening, Father Gill saw a light hovering above the uninhabited section of Mount Pudi. As he watched, the light moved around in the sky very fast and did a number of amazing maneuvers, including right-angle turns. He knew that this was not any type of conventional aircraft. The light then shot up into the sky and was lost in the array of stars. On June 21, that same year, Fathers Gill's assistant Stephen saw what he described as a saucer-shaped object in the sky, hovering above the mission building. In his report concerning the sightings, Father Gill wrote:

"I do not doubt the existence of these things called flying saucers, but my simple mind still requires scientific proof before I can accept that they are from outer space. I am inclined to believe that they are most likely some type of electrical phenomena, or perhaps something brought about by the atom bomb explosions [which were getting blamed for everything in that day, from UFOs to Godzilla]. The fact that Stephen could actually make out a saucer shape could be the work of an overactive imagination, or it is possible that he did see a saucer and they do exist. Yet to me it seems that they may not be solid things."

This was an interesting statement since Father Gill was implying that the objects he saw may not have been any type of craft, but something made of energy. Hynek was under the impression that Gill thought that the objects that were being seen could be living creatures and of a spiritual nature rather than nuts-and-bolts spacecrafts, which was the popular theory at the time. The sightings they had experienced were only a dress rehearsal of what was to follow.

On June 26 at 7:00 p.m., Father Gill saw a bright white light to the northwest while he and thirty to forty other people at the mission watched. A disk-like object that was very large in size stopped and hovered above the mission. He reported that he thought he saw four projections extending from the bottom, and to him they appeared like landing gear. There was a railing or window around the top of the object and as they watched, four human-like figures appeared and seemed to be performing some type of task. As they continued to watch, one or more of the figures would move and disappear and then reappear a few minutes later. A beam of light would periodically project from the center of the craft to the sky; they heard no noise at all. They all watched the object and the beings until about 7:30 p.m., then it ascended into the sky and was lost in the clouds.

An hour later at 8:30 p.m., several smaller objects appeared in the sky and "danced around." They watched these objects until 8:50 p.m., when a larger object came down from the clouds and the smaller objects seemed to go into it. The larger object then rose above the clouds and was no longer visible. Father Gill prepared a written report of what he saw and had most of the people present sign it. The next day at 6:10 p.m., the large object with the beings aboard returned with two of the smaller objects next to it. This extraordinary encounter is described in Father Gill's own words:

"Once again the figures appeared to be doing something on a deck. They looked like they were occasionally bending over and raising their arms, adjusting something. Although I could not tell if they were human or not, they looked like people in the way that they had a head and two arms and legs. One figure seemed to be standing, looking down at us, and when I saw this, I raised my arm to wave at him. To our surprise, the figure did the same and appeared to be waving back to us. We all waved both arms and the figure did the same. There was no doubt that they were responding to us and trying to communicate. We began waving with torches and the object got brighter and dimmer as if responding to the light in the torch fires. The object then moved away, but was visible in the sky as a bright star for several hours after that."

The objects that Father Gill and his companions saw was officially explained by Harvard astronomer Donald Menzel as nothing more than the misinterpretation of the planets Venus and Mars, and although Allen Hynek found this explanation "ludicrous," he kept quiet because at the time he did not want to "rock the boat." In my opinion, this explanation was ridiculous since both planets are merely bright points of light in the sky. Father Gill and the others saw an object with definite structure and intelligent beings out on some type of deck that surrounded the craft. About a year ago, I used a computer astronomy and planetarium program and went back to the day and time of Father Gill's June 26 sighting, and although Venus was low in the west, the planet Mars was not visible at all. Father Gill and the others reported that the object was directly overhead; the location of Venus on the celestial sphere at that time could not account for the sighting.

THE EXETER, NEW HAMPSHIRE, UFO

One of the first major UFO events of the mid-sixties was the sightings made by police and civilians from Exeter, New Hampshire. When I questioned Dr. Hynek about the Exeter UFO case, he said, "This is one of the cases that the Blue Book ignored since they could find no explanation for what took place. I personally investigated it and could not find any natural or conventional cause for these UFO reports."

In 1983, I had the pleasure to meet and work with John G. Fuller. It was John who wrote the first book about this series of sightings, entitled *Incident at Exeter*. John passed away in 1990, but his legacy still inspires paranormal researchers to this day. He was truly a great writer and researcher, and most likely the first to investigate and write about "alien abductions." John and I also worked on a number of projects together, including a television special called *Into the Unknown*, which aired on FOX TV in 1984. The program covered three types of paranormal phenomena including UFOs, metal bending, and faith healing.

During our time together, John and I had many conversations at his home in Weston, Connecticut, and he showed me a great deal of the original investigation material of the UFO/paranormal events that he had researched. When we were discussing UFOs, I brought up the Exeter sightings of 1965 because I had read the book while still in high school and was very interested in what he had to say about the case. John brought out stacks of folders on the case; it was material that never made it into his book because it was considered too bizarre to be accepted at the time. After reading John's material on the Exeter case, I decided to do some investigating of my own. The following is a synopsis of my research of this historic and very complex series of UFO sightings.

On September 3, 1965, after midnight in the early morning hours, police officer Eugene Bertrand of Exeter, New Hampshire, was on routine patrol in the backcountry when he spotted an automobile parked beside the road on Route 101. He stopped to investigate and found a woman in the car crying.

Officer Bertrand asked the woman what was wrong, and she replied that she was chased by an object that was surrounded by a halo of circular red lights. She told the officer that as she tried to get away, the object would make dives toward her car as if it was going to crash into it and then would sweep away at the last moment. She then pointed to a red star in the sky and told Officer Bertrand that the object was still around. To the officer, the light she pointed to seemed like nothing more than a bright star in the sky, so he tried to calm the woman down. After talking with the woman for several minutes, he returned to his police cruiser and drove off, not bothering to make a report or to get the name of the woman.

Thirty minutes later, an eighteen-year-old by the name of Norman Muscarello was hitchhiking along Route 150 in nearby Kensington, returning to his home in Exeter, when he was startled by the appearance of a disk-shaped object with pulsating red lights along its side. The object had risen out of a wooded area, and without a sound it slowly approached Muscarello from no higher than the tops of the trees. The object approached and got about eighty feet from him. He could see a "pool" of bright red light surrounding it, and he estimated that it was approximately one hundred feet in size.

Muscarello became very frightened and ducked behind a stone wall along the side of the road. The object then moved away, and he ran to the nearest house and knocked on the door with the hope of getting someone to view the UFO with him. The home that he went to belonged to a Mr. and Mrs. Russell who did not answer the door, since in his excitement they thought he was drunk or crazy. They had no idea that this was a very scared young man who had just had an encounter with something not of this world.

Muscarello then left the Russell home and walked on foot along the roadway, hoping to catch a ride to Exeter, all the time looking at the sky, hoping the strange object would not come back. He was then picked up by a motorist who saw that the young man was in a terrified state and drove him to the police station at Exeter. The time was about 1:30 a.m. The officer in charge at that hour was Reginald Towland, who later noticed that Muscarello was quite visibly shaken, his complexion was pale, and he could barely stand on his own two feet. After taking his report, Officer Towland radioed to all units advising them to report any strange lights in the sky.

Hearing the call, Officer Bertrand returned to police headquarters and asked Muscarello to take him to the location where he saw the object, a place known as Shaw's Hill. When they arrived at the location, the two sat in the cruiser for several minutes and then decided to get out of the car and proceed toward the field behind the trees where the young man first saw the object rise into the air. They walked for several minutes and saw nothing, then without warning an object rose behind a stand of trees several hundred yards away and began to rise in the air. Bertrand was so shocked at what he saw that he was ready to draw his service revolver to protect them, but he quickly changed his mind. The two men ran back to the police car where Bertrand radioed headquarters and reported his sighting as it was taking place.

After a few minutes, a second police officer joined them, and the three of them continued to watch the object move around in the sky for about ten minutes. They later reported that the UFO was capable of moving from one location to the next at great speed. They reported that the object would accelerate and then stop instantly. The object was red and there was an eerie halo that surrounded it that seemed to make the air glow.

The UFO circled the nearby field without a sound and at times came to within a hundred feet of the two officers and Muscarello. Then it slowly moved away from the three observers, passing over the roadway and disappearing behind the trees in the southeast. As it moved away, they noticed that it rocked back and forth and side to side. It was at this point that they later said that the object behaved more like a living creature than some type of flying machine.

There were several reports of UFOs made that night to local police in the area. A woman from nearby Hampton, New Hampshire, reported that she was "chased by a flying saucer." Also, on a backcountry farm just outside Exeter, a woman called police to say that a "flying saucer" was hovering above her field and shining a light down on her cows. She reported that when she stared at the object, it gave out a flash, which made her face and arms turn red like she had a sunburn. The object then rose straight up in the air and rocked back and forth in the sky. The next day, she went out to the field and found three of her cows dead with "strange" cuts in them and certain parts of their bodies removed as if someone had used a very sharp knife. This encounter was never included in the original case report and was not included in Fuller's book because at the time it sounded too unbelievable to be true, but this may have been one of the first cow/cattle mutilation reports in the northeast United States.

Just hours after the sighting by Muscarello and the two officers at Shaw's Hill, the Exeter police contacted nearby Pease Air Force Base near Portsmouth, New Hampshire, to report the UFO sightings, since they felt it was their duty to relay the information to the proper authorities. The base dispatched two officers, a major and a lieutenant, to investigate the claims. The two Air Force officers went to Shaw's Hill and could find no trace that the object was ever there; however, because of the credibility of the witnesses, they could offer no explanation as to what the object was. In the weeks to follow, more encounters were to take place with some of the witnesses reporting that they felt a connection with the object, a connection they felt was on some psychic level. Some even reported that before the object was visibly seen they could feel its presence. This was something that I would hear over and over again in my investigations of UFOs in the Hudson Valley of New York. The Exeter, New Hampshire, sighting is one of the rare cases in UFO history in which no plausible explanation was offered by the military. There seemed to be no attempt by any government agency to cover up or discredit the sighting, but according to Dr. Hynek, the Air Force went out of its way not to give it any publicity.

THE BETTY AND BARNEY HILL
ALIEN ABDUCTION

While at John Fuller's home, he, to my surprise, allowed me to listen to the actual hypnosis sessions of Barney and Betty Hill, whose UFO abduction case in New Hampshire made headlines across the world during the mid-sixties (fig. 4). The Hill case is without a doubt one of the most puzzling in UFO history, since it may be one of the only UFO abductions that involved a nuts-and-bolts spaceship from another star system. The Barney and Betty Hill story was published in another book by John G. Fuller called *The Interrupted Journey*.

In 1986, I met Betty Hill (Barney passed in February of 1969) at a UFO convention in North Haven, Connecticut, in which we were both speakers. While I was having dinner with Betty, she related to me her experience, something she

Figure 4. Barney and Betty Hill
describe their UFO experience in 1965.

remembered as vividly as the day it took place. The following is a brief account of this most interesting case. The information was obtained through a number of sessions with Betty who, despite having many critics, was still convinced that she and her husband had contact with aliens from another world while driving through the White Mountains in New Hampshire during September of 1961.

BETTY'S STORY

While driving south on U.S. Highway 3 just after 10:00 p.m. on September 19, 1961, the Hills noticed a bright star in the sky that seemed to follow them for many miles. The light then changed course and looked like it was heading right for them, getting brighter and brighter with each passing moment. Betty mentioned that it was a UFO, but Barney, somewhat skeptical, said to his wife, "Don't be foolish. It's probably an aircraft or a satellite." When the light continued to follow, Betty grabbed the binoculars from the back seat to take a look at this mysterious light in the sky. Betty said that she saw an object that had a double row of lights around it.

The object continued to approach the Hills' car, and then it stopped above a number of trees less than one hundred feet away. Barney then stopped the car and got out to take a look for himself. He described what he saw as a large, glowing pancake-shaped object, and at that point he was sure that it was some type of top-secret military aircraft. As Barney continued to look, he said to Betty, "How interesting. The pilot of the craft is looking at me." He then saw three others also looking at him from what appeared to be windows around the edge of the object. Barney became terrified, thinking these people might want to hurt them because he saw a top-secret military weapon, so the Hills got back into their car and raced away. Then they heard a strange beeping sound, which made them feel very drowsy. The next thing they remembered was hearing the beeping sound once again and becoming fully alert. They were surprised and then confused to notice that they were now several miles south from where they saw the UFO. They expected to arrive home at three in the morning, but found that it was after 5:00 a.m.; somehow, some way, they had lost two hours of conscious time.

STRANGE, SHINY CIRCLES

The next day, Betty went out to the car and discovered over a dozen shiny circles scattered on the trunk. Each circle was about an inch in diameter and perfectly round. When a compass was placed near each spot, the needle spun wildly, indicating a strong magnetic field. The Hills then filed a report with Pease Air Force Base in Portsmouth just thirty-six hours after the incident.

Shortly after the encounter, Betty became obsessed with UFOs and tried to read as much material as she could to better understand what had happened to them. The Hills both began experiencing psychological and physical effects shortly after the encounter. Betty had nightmares almost every night about being taken out of the car and taken aboard a spacecraft by small, human-like alien beings with large heads. Barney began to suffer from high blood pressure, ulcers, and a strange circular rash, which appeared around his groin area. Both Hills underwent extensive medical examinations and were eventually referred to Dr. Benjamin Simon, a well-respected psychiatrist and neurologist with a background in regressive hypnosis therapy.

THE DOCTOR

Betty told me that she and Barney were in therapy for several months at the Hills' own expense. Under hypnosis, they told identical stories on how their car stalled and they were surrounded by a number of little humanoid men dressed in tight-fitting uniforms. They were then taken aboard a craft and both were given physical examinations by an alien being that she called the doctor. Barney was frightened, so the beings made him docile with some type of tranquilizer, and after her exam by the "doctor," Betty was taken on a brief tour of the ship. When she asked where they were from, she was shown a star map. Betty was then told that they would not remember being taken aboard the craft, and the couple was released back to their car.

The last thing that Betty consciously remembers is seeing the UFO moving away high in the sky, appearing finally like a bright red-orange ball of fire. The Hills' encounter was known only to a small number of people at the time, but that was soon to change when, in 1966, the magazine *Look* published a two-part excerpt from John Fuller's *The Interrupted Journey*. Because of the publicity from the magazine, the book became a bestseller. I first read the Hills' story in *Look*, and although I was only about sixteen years old, it fueled my interest in UFOs even more. It still amazes me to think that about twenty years later, after reading the book and the *Look* article, I would be working with John G. Fuller, the man who wrote *The Interrupted Journey*, and having dinner with the most famous UFO abductee of all time, Betty Hill.

THE STORY CONTINUES

During one of my many visits to John's home, we began discussing the Hill case, and once again he let me listen to the original tapes made by Dr. Simon during his sessions with both Hills using hypnosis. I listened to the voice of Barney, who was terrified, and then listened to the voice of Betty describing under hypnosis the beings in the spaceship. I must admit it sent chills up and down my spine. If they were faking it, then both Hills should have won Academy Awards.

In 1975, the Hill case became even more popular when a TV movie called *The UFO Incident* was made about their experience. The two-hour movie was broadcast at prime time and starred Estelle Parsons as Betty Hill and James Earl Jones as Barney. My connection with the Hill case does not end there. In 2000, Estelle Parsons's son became a student in my class and, knowing my interest in UFOs, we had a brief discussion during a parent-teacher conference about the role she played as Betty Hill. Coincidence? Later I would have more meetings with Betty, and some of them turned out very strange, indicating that she still had some type of connection with an intelligence that was not of this world. Betty passed over in October of 2004, which was a great loss to the UFO community.

Recently, a once-classified Air Force document was recovered using the Freedom of Information Act, which may give more support to the Hill case. The document told of a radar sighting of an unknown object by the SAC 100th Bomb Wing at the exact same time and location of the Hill sighting.

THE HUDSON VALLEY UFO MYSTERY

On June 25, 2007, I spoke at a UFO conference in the Greenwich Village area of New York City. The event was hosted by *UFO Magazine* and the NYC-based organization SPACE, which stands for Search Project for Aspects of Close Encounters. SPACE was founded in 1992, and it was one of the very few groups made up of people who have had a close encounter. The members get together, share their experiences, gather information and research, and make it available to the public. The group also invites others who have had an experience with a UFO to contact them. A great majority of the members actually had experiences in the Hudson Valley region close to the towns of Southeast and Brewster, New York. One of the founders of SPACE, Harold Egeln, is a longtime associate of mine who has had personal paranormal experiences and has used his insight to assist me on a number of investigations in the past. Harold's encounters with UFO-related phenomena appears in chapter 10. If you would like to contact SPACE, the address of the organization's Web page can be found in the appendix of this book. Also at the conference were two fellow researchers who I hadn't seen in a while, Paul Greco and Francine Vale. Paul is a UFO investigator who runs a MUFON group in Yonkers, New York, and Francine is a healer and spiritual teacher who has impressive insight into the unseen world.

As I began my PowerPoint presentation, I asked the audience (which numbered about 150), if anyone had ever had a UFO sighting, and in response more than half the people in the room raised their hands. Then when I asked how many actually reported the sighting or talked about it with someone else, all the hands went down except for a few. I then asked how many had read my book *Night Siege: The Hudson Valley UFO Sightings* and knew something or heard about the thousands of sightings in that location from 1983 through 1995. To my surprise, only about twenty people in the room raised their hands. This was somewhat of a shock to me since the Hudson Valley is only about twenty-five miles north of New York City, and during the eighties, the UFO reports were well publicized in radio, television, and newspapers, including the *New York Times*.

The UFO sightings that took place in the Hudson Valley area of New York between 1983 and 1985 add up to perhaps one of the greatest of all the classic UFO cases (fig. 5, the Hudson Valley UFO). Thousands of people from all walks of life had an encounter with an object that was reported to be the size of a football field. This object hovered over major highways and stopped traffic as hundreds of motorists looked up to see a brightly lit object that was described as being like a city in the sky. These sightings were very important to me because I was the chief investigator and it was my first "big" case, and I will remember what took place during those years for the rest of my life.

Figure 5. Hudson Valley UFO over
Waterbury, Connecticut, May 1987.

One of the main reasons why this series of UFO events
made such an impression on me is because my entire investigation team and I witnessed the UFO on three separate occasions. (My sightings of the object are documented in *Night
Siege*.) During the peak of the sightings, there were all types
of encounters taking place from lights in the sky to closer encounters that involved abductions and contact with some type
of nonhuman intelligence. The Hudson Valley UFO sightings
were parts of the first real, major case in which the triangular
and boomerang-shaped UFOs made their grand appearance.

Normally when UFOs are seen over a long period of time
and witnessed by thousands, the event has a rational explanation, but in this case there was none. To this day, the Hudson Valley UFOs remain a mystery. It is beyond the scope of
this book to present this case in detail; I will only present
some of the reports and update the information so that my

readers can get a feel of what a UFO outbreak (called a flap) is like and how these sightings relate to the rest of this book. Before you can even begin to understand what the true nature of the UFOs represents, you must be educated in the phenomenon itself and my part in its investigation.

MARCH 24, 1983: A NIGHT TO REMEMBER

March 24, 1983, was a night many residents of the Hudson River Valley will not soon forget. Just how many people actually saw the large, boomerang-shaped object as it drifted over the major highways and homes during a three hour period that evening will probably never be known. It wasn't just the sheer number that was astounding—all of the reports confirmed that something alien to the world as we know it appeared over one of the most heavily populated areas in the United States. It was staging a remarkable display in the sky as a multitude of witnesses just stared upward to watch the mostly silent apparition drift by.

There was, for example, the doctor and his family who saw a white beam of light come down from the object and then saw a small red object travel halfway down the beam and shoot across to the horizon. There was the couple who described the object as having a massive structure at least six stories high. More astonishing, they said it shot to the far horizon and came right back to a hovering position near them again—all in a split second. There was the woman driving alone who saw the object quite a distance away, then a second later, right over her car. There was the president of a data-processing company who saw a red light jump from one part of the object to another. There was the family of four who became frightened as they watched the object hover over the road. They sped underneath it to get away from it, and as they did, a beam of light engulfed the car, causing one of the children to feel a tingling sensation. There was the aircraft designer who saw the lights about a hundred yards away suddenly break formation, with the outside lights moving to the inside and the inside lights going to the outside. There were many people who saw the object simply disappear in an instant, often to reappear a moment later in a blinding flash of lights.

One of the most surprising things I learned was that residents of two communities fifteen miles apart saw a similar object at the same time and for a considerable length of time. This indicated to me that there were at least two different objects in the Hudson Valley that night. Both were boomerang-shaped and huge with a brilliant array of multicolored lights surrounding some type of dark structure. Of all the sightings reported from the March 24 event, 87 percent came from the area of Westchester and Putnam Counties, only three miles wide and twelve miles long. The Taconic State Parkway runs through the center of this part of southern New York, and the object appeared to have been meandering back and forth in a helix-like pattern using the roadway as a center post.

The first reported sighting came at 7:30 p.m. from Hunt Middleton, an executive of a major New York City corporation. Hunt had just stepped off a commuter bus in Bedford, and as he walked toward his home, he saw lights in the sky through the bare branches of trees lining the sidewalk.

"I'm not sure how many lights, perhaps six or seven, but they were very bright. They were all blinking on and off and were red, blue, green, and white. I knew it was not any type of conventional aircraft because the lights were stationary; it was just hovering there in the sky. I tried listening for a sound but heard nothing. The lights looked like they were in a straight line, but you could tell they extended around in sort of a half circle. I continued to watch for five minutes, and all this time the object did not move. I finally went inside my house to get my family to come out and see it, but when we came out the lights were gone."

Bedford, New York, is in the southern part of the twelve-mile-long "sighting zone." Other witnesses from the same area said the object was heading north. If it had continued in that direction, it would have gone over Yorktown, one of the most heavily populated communities in Westchester County. Yet no sightings were reported from Yorktown until around 8:30 p.m., about an hour later, and as far as we can determine, there were no sightings anywhere for a full half-hour after the Bedford sighting. The question that puzzled me was, where does an object that size go and hide for at least a half-hour? Could it have been invisible during that time? Or perhaps the answer was that this was not a physical object (as we understand the words *physical* and *matter*), but something else that was able to slide between the dimensions of space and time.

The next reported sighting was at 8:00 p.m. in the small town of Carmel, ten miles north of Bedford. Steve Wittles, a computer consultant in his thirties, was entertaining three friends at his home when he looked out a window and noticed red and white lights in a half circle, hovering over trees several hundred yards away. Wittles and his guests ran outside and watched. They thought they could see the vague outline of something connecting the lights. Despite its size, the object made no sound that they could hear. After a minute or so, it began to drift toward the east and went out of sight beyond some trees.

Just moments later and about a quarter of a mile to the east, Dr. Lawrence Greenman and his wife, Joan, and their three daughters got an even better look at it. They had been watching television at the time. Mrs. Greenman told Dr. Hynek and myself, "I saw a very bright object come from the north-northwest, and after a few seconds I got off the couch and went outside to see what it was. My husband and children went with me. We were looking west and there was this huge object. I went back inside to get binoculars, and when I came back it had stopped in midair and was hovering over the trees. I looked at it through the binoculars and saw just a group of lights in a straight line. The lights seemed to be in a pattern like a zigzag. As I looked through the binoculars, I saw some type of metallic rod connecting the lights of a dull green color. The object turned a little bit, and I could see that it was a wide V-shape. I then saw a very brilliant white beam of light come down from the center, and in that bright light a small, reddish object came down and headed very, very fast toward the north. Then the beam of light shut off, and whatever this thing was, it started to move very slowly toward the south and then turned and went east."

A number of sightings then took place at the same time in the towns of Millwood and Yorktown in Westchester County, and in Kent and Brewster in Putnam County. Although there were only a handful of reports from the Kent-Brewster area there were far more witnesses in Millwood and Yorktown— well over a thousand people is a conservative estimate.

Joan Lindauer's report was typical of those I received from the Millwood area. An employee of GTE at the time, in White Plains, she was en route to her home in Croton, driving on Route 120 toward the Taconic Parkway, when she saw a group of lights just hanging in the sky. She assumed they belonged to an aircraft heading for the Westchester County Airport, several miles northeast of White Plains.

"I thought it was an aircraft, but it didn't keep going toward the airport; it either stayed still or kept going the other way. Then I noticed that it was going parallel to me, so low that I lost it at times behind the trees. Then I came to a location where the sky was open, and I got my first good look at the lights in the sky. It was at least the size of a large jet, with brilliant white lights in the shape of a V. It kept following me all the way to Millwood. I started to get scared and tried to convince myself it was just a plane, but it didn't act like one. As I approached Millwood at the intersection of Route 133, I stopped at the traffic light. As I did, the object sped up and swung in front of my car and hovered right above the traffic light. Then the lights on the object went from all white to all red. It was very, very low. It was just right there. There was no one else at the intersection, and here was this thing hovering several hundred feet above the light without making a sound. The traffic light finally turned green and I just left. I didn't want to watch anymore. I thought I was going crazy."

The UFO now headed north and followed the Taconic Parkway, where it caused a traffic disturbance. Cars stopped on both sides of the expressway and puzzled motorists got out to look at the mysterious object drifting soundlessly overhead. Many of them reported seeing a beam of brilliant white light that occasionally came down from the bottom of the object and engulfed people and cars. Ed Burns, at the time an IBM program manager and a resident of Yorktown Heights, was driving north when he spotted the formation of lights off to his right.

"As I continued to drive, the lights became more profound, and then they came right over my car. I shut the radio off, rolled the window down, and looked out at this huge craft above me. I heard no noise. It was moving silently and slowly. When I reached the Millwood area, I noticed twelve cars off to the side of the road. I pulled over and stopped, and then all of a sudden this huge craft was right over my car. That's when it was really shocking. Then the craft seemed to stop. The different colored lights seemed to go off, and just the white lights seemed to stay on. It was hovering a bit. It was just there looking like it was observing us as we were observing it. This craft was there a minute or two, and then it started to move again, going up the Taconic Parkway in a sort of a Z pattern. It seemed to be going very slowly, and then all of a sudden it seemed like it was very far ahead of me. The object appeared to be triangular in shape and had lights all around it with thirty to forty colored lights along the back alone. If there is such a thing as a flying city, this was a flying city. It was not a small craft. It was huge."

About the same time, the Yorktown police began receiving the first of dozens of phone calls from excited residents. At one point, the object hovered over the center of town, where police officer Kevin Soravilla saw it. He thought it was a jetliner in trouble, but as he watched, he realized the object wasn't a plane. It turned 180 degrees around, as if on a wheel, and slowly drifted away. Soravilla was excited, and he radioed headquarters to report what he had seen. He was told by the station dispatcher that they were getting quite a few calls; in fact, the police were becoming concerned because all the lines were being tied up by calls about the UFO. Traffic was snarled on major streets as people stopped to look up as the UFO passed overhead. The same thing was happening on the Taconic Parkway as people pulled over and got out of their cars to watch.

One of the most impressive sightings from the Taconic Parkway area came from Bill Hele, at that time the chief meteorologist for the National Weather Corporation. He is a trained observer who is familiar with all types of aircraft, yet he could not identify what it was he saw that night. Whatever it was, he said, it was "as large as an aircraft carrier."

Hele was driving south on the parkway when lights appeared on the horizon in the vicinity of the Westchester County Airport. "They weren't moving very fast, but they were extremely bright and it aroused my curiosity. I went down a hill and up to the crest of the next, and at that point I was beginning to become concerned as to what it could be. I was curious enough to pull my car off the road. I got out and took another look at this thing. I have been around planes for the past twenty years—and at that point I realized that this thing did not have the appearance of any known object or anything similar to an airplane or group of airplanes that I'd ever seen.

"I began to study this series of six or seven lights coming at me. The appearance of the lights was like a large check mark or a V with one end of the V clipped off. As the object approached, there was no sound. I estimate the initial altitude to be less than two thousand feet. As it approached, it seemed to be lowering to approximately one thousand feet. Soon it was at about a forty-five-degree angle to me away from the ground and away from the moon, which was full. The object slowed down, not to a stop but nearly to a crawl, still moving. All the lights were changing color at a different time frame from the other lights, as if it had a rotating prism within the lights. No aircraft I've ever seen has a rotating prism for a light source. At this point, all the lights on the horizontal axis ceased to exist, the way you would see the incandescence of a light shrink to zero lumens as it went out, in perhaps a fifth of a second. After not hearing a sound and seeing absolutely nothing in the sky except stars, I was amazed to find not even a silhouette of an object. That had me not exactly frightened, but on the verge. I'm searching the heavens all around me, up and down and to the side, for thirty to forty seconds, and I'm looking up when all of a sudden, flash! The entire string of lights came on. I looked back at my VW, beginning to become a little frightened. I was beginning to feel that if something happened to me out here, who would even know or wonder why I had disappeared? However, I continued to stare at it. It was about one thousand feet above me, and it subtended an arc in the sky that led me to believe that perhaps I was looking at a series of lights about a quarter of a mile long.

"The object continued to hover for half a dozen seconds and then slowly began to drift northward parallel to the parkway. Then a strange thing happened. All the lights seemed to be still pointing right at me, or focused on me, and the coloration turned to a slimy green, a computer green. It slowly drifted off across the horizon. About this time, two young men came running up to me and in hysterical voices asked me if I had a camera. I had to calm them down. They said they'd been chasing the object through Yorktown and had never seen anything like it in their lives."

Another excellent witness was Dennis Fleming, president of International Information Services Limited, a data-processing company in Greenwich, Connecticut. He saw the object twice while driving north along the parkway and twice more from his home in Croton Manor.

"I noticed four lights on the horizon and slowed down to get a better look," explained Fleming, whose background is in aviation and air-traffic control systems. "The car in front of me was weaving in and out of the lanes and slowing down and speeding up. It looked like he was looking at the lights. I then pulled to the side of the road and stopped. My first reaction was that this thing was very big. There was no sound. Any aircraft that large should have been heard, no matter how noisy the Taconic was at the time. I stopped and got out of the car. It was very quiet there, and this time I heard the object. It sounded like a very small single-engine aircraft. It was very faint with a moderate pitch. It was almost like the puttering sound on a motorboat engine. I then rushed home and told my children and we looked at the object through a telescope. We still could not see any structure at all. We lost it in the distance going toward Peekskill. Later, I tried objectively to explain what I saw, but I could not. I read in the paper the next day that quite a few people saw it, and it was, I think, something great. I was especially interested when other people described the same things that I did."

SIGHTINGS IN PUTNAM COUNTY, NEW YORK

At the same time that the sightings were taking place along the Taconic, other people were seeing a similar object fifteen miles to the north in Putnam County near the communities of Kent, Carmel, Lake Carmel, and Brewster. However, the Putnam object seemed to be somewhat smaller than the one being seen in Westchester County, and many of the sightings in Putnam were close encounters; that is, the object came within five hundred feet or so of the observers.

At eight thirty that evening, James Holtsman, his wife, Ruth, and their two sons, James Jr., eighteen, and Martin, thirteen, were returning to their home in Kent on Route 301 after visiting a relative in nearby Cold Spring when they noticed a series of white lights hovering about three hundred feet above the road ahead of them. The lights were in a boomerang pattern and were red, green, blue, and white. They were so bright they lit the tops of the trees. Holtsman stopped and got out of the car. "The strange thing about it," he told me later, "was that the object made no sound. It just hung there motionless in the sky. It was like seeing a ghost."

At this time, another car approached from the opposite direction and stopped almost underneath the object. The driver got out and looked up at the UFO. As he did, the lights suddenly began flashing in a crazy sequence up and down the "wings," at which time the man jumped back in his car, quickly turned around, and sped off in the direction from which he had come. Now the object began to move slowly toward the Holtsman car, frightening Mrs. Holtsman and the boys. They pleaded with Holtsman to get back in the car and get out of there. This he did, and as he stepped on the gas and passed underneath the object, the car was bathed in a blinding white light for a brief moment, causing young Martin's skin to tingle. They sped away in their car, not looking back, and headed for home.

The object's apparent fascination with lakes and ponds attracted the attention of David Miller, an artist who was driving north on a road near Brewster, also at about 8:30 p.m. He had seen white lights on the horizon several minutes earlier and then had lost sight of them because of trees.

"I proceeded about a mile or so more and I passed a very large pond close to my home. I was startled to see the object hovering right above the pond," Miller told us. "The pond is right next to the road, and I would say the object was about 200 feet from the road, and no more than 120 feet above the water. This object was very large. When I first looked at it, I saw the white strobe lights that I had seen before, and then two searchlights went on. They were quite large, white in color, and they seemed to be coming from the southern end. These searchlights moved across the surface of the pond as if the object was looking for something. These lights were very bright. I stopped my car to watch. As I was watching the object sweep the beams of light across the water, I could hear a very faint whooshing sound."

At about the same time, several dozen people in a restaurant at a ski slope near Stormville saw a formation of white lights in a boomerang shape hover over a utility pole about two hundred yards away. What they didn't know was that at that same moment several people were looking up at the UFO from near the base of the pole.

John Piccone, a Yorktown resident with an aerospace background, noticed an unusual feature when he and his wife and their fourteen-year-old son watched the object approach their house at about 8:45 p.m.

"It came over the trees and circled our place twice. At first I thought it was an aircraft, but judging by the way it was flying, I ruled this out immediately. It flew very smooth and the sound coming from it was very quiet. I should have heard much more sound than I did. I've been working around aircraft for a long time, and I don't know any aircraft engine that is quiet like that. I judged its altitude at about 1,500 feet. Single-engine aircraft would have made quite a sound. The object passed over our driveway, and it was kind of like a V formation. One of the lights from the right side of the formation pulled away and backed off a bit. It almost seemed as if it was observing us. Ten or twenty seconds later, it pulled back into formation. I work on spacecraft as well as aircraft; there is no doubt in my mind that what I saw was not conventional aircraft."

The next reported sighting came from the village of New Castle, six miles south of Yorktown in Westchester County. As the object passed over New Castle, it left a trail of amazed, and sometimes frightened, people. The New Castle police began receiving phone calls about 9:00 p.m. At first, the dispatcher, not knowing what to think, dismissed the reports. But calls continued to come in, and officers were sent out to investigate. By then, one officer on patrol, Andy Sadoff, was already looking at the object. Sadoff at that time was a New Castle policewoman for over five years, and she was in a radar car parked in a driveway on Cross Ridge Road, on the lookout for speeders. To her left was a large hill that partially obstructed that part of the sky.

"All of a sudden from over the hill I saw a string of white lights, very large, forming a half circle. It was just coming over the ridge and it caught my attention because it was so large. It then turned left and started coming around to where I was parked. I started shaking my head, thinking that this was strange because I heard no sound and this thing was huge. It then passed over my vehicle and headed toward the town. Then about four minutes later, it came back in my direction. It turned toward my car once again, but this time it was much lower. The way the object moved was very smooth, as if it was gliding. When it came around I could see the shape better. It was in the shape of a V with white lights on the top and green lights on the bottom. It was flying toward me and heading right for my car. So I looked out the window and did the normal thing, I locked the doors.

"This time it was very low. I stuck my head out the window, and it stopped right over my car. It then hovered there about twenty seconds, and I could see a mass that was very large. Behind the lights, I could see a large solid object. There was still no sound at all, and I'm saying to myself, 'This can't be happening. What's happening here?' So I got on my radio and made a call to one of the other guys, and they said they got quite a few calls about it. The object then started to move once again and headed over the ridge, and I lost sight of it."

One of the most dramatic sightings of the Hudson Valley UFO was to take place almost a year later when the triangular-boomerang UFO hovered above the Indian Point nuclear reactor. The sighting was confirmed by the complex's spokesperson, and this was the first report of a confirmation of a UFO over a restricted area. Fifteen minutes before the Indian Point nuclear reactor complex sighting, the UFO was videotaped as it passed over Brewster, New York. The videotape was looked at by imaging scientists at the Jet Propulsion Laboratory in Pasadena, California, and found to be one solid object of immense size.

The Hudson Valley sightings continued into the 1990s, but many of the encounters were contact experiences. Just about all the people who felt some type of psychic connection with the UFO later would claim to have been abducted by the intelligence behind the UFO or would claim some type of contact. This is an important fact to remember, since it explains why UFOs concentrate on certain geographic locations and then move on.

THE GULF BREEZE, FLORIDA, SIGHTINGS

Gulf Breeze is a little town of less than ten thousand located in the Florida panhandle. It has always been a quiet place to live and dependent on the tourists visiting its sandy beaches in the spring, fall, and winter; however, residents of this sleepy little town would have never guessed that it would become one of the most famous UFO capitals of the world.

On November 11, 1987, Ed Walters, a local contractor and resident, was outside his home when he saw a glowing object that was partially hidden by a pine tree in his front yard. Ed then went to investigate, trying to get a clear view of the sky by walking to the side of the tree. He then saw a top-shaped craft with a row of lights around it hovering in the sky. The object had a bright luminous ring around the bottom and it seemed to be about fifty feet above the road. He ran to grab his Polaroid camera and took several pictures from his front yard. He then saw a bright blue beam of light, which shot out of the craft, stunning him, raising him several feet above the ground, and dropping him. He then heard a voice in his head say, "Don't worry, we will not harm you." He passed out and when he awoke several minutes later, the UFO was gone.

About a week later, he went to the local newspaper and presented the photographs to the news editor for publication and told him of the strange events that led to the images on the film. The editor of the paper published the story and photos, and soon after it was picked up by the major news wire services. Almost overnight, Gulf Breeze had become the UFO capital of the world.

At first Ed Walters hid his identity, but he later went public with more photographs and stories of UFO encounters. In the months and years to follow, many more people would report seeing UFOs in the Gulf Breeze area, giving considerable credibility to Walters's claim. Many of these people reported to have had sightings before Mr. Walters, but kept their stories quiet for fear of ridicule. It was only after the Walters photographs and story appeared in the newspaper and on television that they decided to come forward with their own sighting accounts. Yes, Gulf Breeze had become the mecca for UFO sightseers as hundreds flocked down to the sleepy little town in the hope of seeing a flying saucer or, even better, get some good video footage that could be sold to the tabloids.

In 1987, I was interviewed by NBC News about UFOs and was asked about the Gulf Breeze sightings. I answered that I was not sure if they were all authentic and that UFO researchers must be open to the fact that at least some of the reports might be a clever hoax. When the story hit the airwaves with my comments, they came across sounding like I believed that all the sightings in Gulf Breeze were the product of hoaxers and publicity seekers. In the days to follow I received several calls from well-known UFO investigators who were very angry at me for voicing my opinion. Since then I have learned to watch what I say, because when it comes to UFO research, there are too many egos out there trying to compete. If the Walters photographs were faked, it didn't stop him from becoming somewhat of a celebrity, and he even made a number of appearances on several major prime-time television shows.

Walters then sold his house and it was purchased by a Mr. Robert E. Menzer. While cleaning the attic, a model spaceship was found that looked like the UFO in Ed Walters's photographs. The model was nine inches long and five inches deep. It was made of two nine-inch foam plates attached to two six-inch foam plates. A six-inch square of blue plastic film was attached to the bottom of the model on a six-inch round orange paper ring. The windows were drawn on the model. When the story made the press, Walters rebutted by saying that it was a setup and only a fool would leave the model behind. However, discounting the possibility that the Walters photos were a hoax, I felt that there were still a great number of real UFO sightings in that section of Florida.

MY VISIT TO GULF BREEZE

In the mid-1990s I was invited to Gulf Breeze by the local chapter of the Mutual UFO Network (MUFON). I was surprised how great the interest in UFOs was and how many people in that small town close to Pensacola had encounters of all kinds. Although it was August and hot, it didn't stop me from traveling around asking questions and interviewing people who had a sighting or a close encounter. From the information that I gathered, it seemed that dozens of people would convene at a number of pier locations or on the beach and set up cameras in the hope of catching something on film. I did attend two of these sessions in different parts of the town, but I did it incognito. At that time I was a well-known researcher and I didn't want to get barraged by questions from UFO enthusiasts. During the three days and nights that I was there, I spent a great deal of time with a number of people who were out to get an evening thrill by looking for flying saucers. I must admit that mostly what appeared on those nights seemed like aircraft in the distance, their lights being distorted by the temperature inversions from the heat rising off the land and being pushed out to the Gulf of Mexico.

There was one sighting that I had with a group of people that was unexplained. A ball of light appeared in the southwest and it approached our location at about a seventy-five-degree angle. The light was a light yellow, a single light, and as it approached at its highest point in the sky it was as bright as the planet Venus would appear as a morning or evening star (this, my friends, is quite bright). However, the object was not star-like, but a sphere of light. It then stopped and hovered for about thirty seconds and just hung in the sky like a lantern attached to some imaginary wire. Needless to say, it created a great deal of excitement in the group. The light then did about ten figure-eight loops and moved away to the north. As it did, it appeared to be getting fainter as if it was increasing in altitude. The time of this sighting was about 11:00 p.m., and as far as I was concerned this was the only unusual object that I saw. The rest of the lights that we saw that night that were also labeled as UFOs were, in my opinion, conventional aircraft and perhaps a few satellites that passed overhead.

STITCHES AND UFOS

The next day, I decided to relax and take a swim in the Gulf of Mexico. Since I was staying at a beachfront hotel in Gulf Breeze, I took full advantage of the warm water. To make a long story short, I injured myself on some coral rock close to the shore. It made a deep gash in my foot, which was bleeding quite profusely. I was directed to the local hospital in Gulf Breeze, which was one floor with a small emergency room. The nurse came up to me and took my insurance and other information and told me that the doctor would be right with me. I sat in the chair for several minutes, and then the doctor came over and introduced himself. He looked at the medical form, which had my name and other information, and then just stared at me for what seemed a very long period of time. At that point I started getting worried. I thought, *Am I going into shock or something? Why is he staring at me?* The doctor then asked me if I was involved with UFOs, and I said yes. He then ran back to the reception desk and said, "Hey everybody, come here. Remember that book I read about UFOs and passed around? Well, the guy who wrote it is here in my emergency room!" He was in fact referring to *Night Siege: The Hudson Valley UFO Sightings* (first edition). At that point, I was surrounded by just about everyone on duty in the ER and was signing autographs and answering questions. Well, I finally got treated, received ten stitches, and was told to give the foot a rest and keep it elevated.

One of the great things about that visit that made it worth the laceration and stitches is that I collected a number of UFO sightings from personnel in the hospital. Although most of them were of vague lights in the sky, there was one made by a nurse who, just two years before my visit to Gulf Breeze, had an experience that changed her life. The name of the nurse is being withheld; however, for the purpose of this report, I will refer to her as "Mary." The next day, despite my injury, I met with Mary at her home in Gulf Breeze. The following is a transcript from what was told to me that day in August.

MARY'S STORY

"I have only been in this area for just over two years. I originally came from California and the way I got here was because of some type of alien intelligence. Let me start from the beginning because I think it has bearing on my story. When I was a child, I used to look up at the stars and tell everyone that's where I came from. My parents thought it was just a childhood game, but I really believed it. During many nights until I was about twelve years old, I would wake up in the middle of the night, two or three in the morning, to find a glowing being standing by my bed. I could not tell if it was a man or woman, perhaps a little of both. The being that I was sure was an angel would smile at me, and through its eyes I could tell that it was communicating with me, putting information in my head. I did not hear any type of voice; I just heard a vibrating buzzing sound, which eventually gave me a headache. When I was brought to the point where I started showing pain, the being would stop and then disappear, only to repeat the same thing at least twice a month for several years. As time went on, I become more and more psychic, not that I could read minds, but I could sense what people were feeling, which gave me an understanding of the pain felt in others. I think this is why I became a nurse.

"I had a number of UFO sightings when I was a teenager and adult, but until I was thirty I never had what you would call a close encounter. During the week of June 21 in 1990, I was feeling very uneasy, as if someone were watching me. These were the types of feelings that I would get as a child on the nights the 'angel' would come into my room. I lived in a small rented house just outside Venice Beach, California and it was quite isolated. The night of June 23, I went to bed and was awaken by a blue light in the room and a buzzing sound that vibrated my head. I tried to sit up in bed but could not move my body. I could only move my eyes around and saw the same being that I witnessed as a child walk right through the wall. I heard a voice in my right ear say, 'Hello Mary, we have come for you. Do not fear us. Do you accept me?' I didn't know what to say, so I said yes.

"The being then raised his hand, and I floated off the bed and started moving toward the wall. I was afraid I was going to crash into it when a vortex-like tunnel appeared and I went through it. The next thing I knew I was standing in a large room. The light was so bright in this room that I had to shield my eyes, so it was difficult to see anything around me in the glare. I did see a number of people who were very human and some were not. I saw a number of beings that looked like the 'angel' and one of them came over to me and said, 'This is a gathering point from all around creation, of beings that we communicate with and help.'

"I was led to a large room that could have been hundreds of stories high and along the sides were millions of cylinders.

The 'angel' told me that they collect DNA from races that are endangered from all around this universe, other universes, and other dimensions. They do this to preserve the races and to improve them so that one day they can join with the creator of all things. I was told that my DNA was selected and that my children are also located in this room, sleeping, waiting to be born and seeded on other worlds. I then yelled at this being and said, 'What gives you the right to do this!' He replied, 'Survival of all living things. Besides, you agreed to help us with this task a very long time ago.'

"The angelic being then told me that we were at our destination. I then started feeling dizzy and there was a bright light. I was then on a beach with a number of people and two of the 'angels.' It was night and very hot, the sand was a pure white, and at first I thought I was on another planet, but the being seemed to read my thoughts and told me I was still on Earth. He said that this place is where a great number of the people who they work with live, and someday I will be here also. He said, 'We implant a memory or desire in the minds of those we work with at a very early age to move to this location.' I did not know where I was, but I knew now it was on Earth, somewhere in the southern part of the United States. I was shown a number of locations where they had bases and areas where there were secret vortexes, or 'gates' as they are called, to other worlds and dimensions. The 'angel' then waved his hands across my eyes, and the next thing I knew, I woke up in bed. In the next few days I had the desire to find out where I was, the white sand was the key. It's here at Gulf Breeze and Pensacola; this is where the angel brought me. I have been here for two years and have met a number of people who also had the same experience and moved here for the same reasons."

I stayed as long as I could in Gulf Breeze, but I had to leave and head back to Connecticut. I kept in contact with Mary for several months and then lost touch; she seemed to have vanished off the face of the earth. She no longer worked in the hospital at Gulf Breeze, and they had no forwarding address. In the months and years to follow, I met a number of other people, who like Mary had a desire to head down to that area of the United States. Most claim it was a strong feeling, others claimed it was the result of a "dream" as a child.

THE BELGIUM UFOS

During 1989 and into the early nineties, the small country of Belgium was besieged by UFO sightings. What's interesting about this case is that it involved a boomerang or triangular UFO, almost identical to the object seen in the Hudson Valley of New York a number of years earlier. At this time I was considered an "expert" on triangular UFOs, and because of the similarities between the two incidents the researchers in Belgium often contacted me for advice, and they would frequently send me their reports for my opinion. One of the drawbacks was that everything was in French, and I had to get a translator to read the material so that I could find out what was going on. The Belgium area is geographically much like the Hudson Valley of New York, and what took place there was almost a carbon copy of the sightings that took place earlier an ocean away.

On November 29, 1989, in Eupen, Belgium, two police officers were on patrol when they saw a dark, triangular object with three bright lights on its underside shining to the ground. The object also had a red light in the middle, which turned from red to orange. The object was about two hundred yards from the side of the road and at an altitude of four hundred feet. As the officers watched in wonderment, the object changed direction and passed directly over their heads. The only sound that was heard was a soft electrical-like hum. The UFO then moved over the Gileppe Dam and hovered there for thirty minutes. Finally it disappeared as it headed toward the town of Spa.

The officers contacted the Belgium Air Force at Bierset, which told them that they had tracked the object on radar. The sightings continued in the Spa area, where the object was witnessed by countless people and nineteen police officers. About an hour later, the same two Eupen police officers saw another object, much larger, come over the trees next to the location in which they were parked. It slowly lowered in altitude and they could tell it was triangular in shape. The object then turned, rotated, and flew away following the main road at about forty-five miles an hour.

On March 30, 1990, in Wavre, Belgium, at about 11:00 p.m., the local police began receiving calls of a giant triangular object in the sky with bright lights. The police reported the sightings to the radar station at Glons, where the object was confirmed on radar. The radar operators said that the object was at an altitude of three thousand feet, and it was like no aircraft that they had ever seen before. The sighting and radar confirmation were reported to the Belgium Air Force, and wing commander Colonel Wilfried de Brouwer gave the order to scramble two F-16 fighters from Beauvechain. The F-16 interceptors detected a positive image on their radar that was oval-shaped; however, they could see nothing visually. The F-16 pilots attempted to lock onto the object with their onboard radar system—their purpose was not to fire a missile, but to get verification that this was a real, solid object in the sky. As soon as a radar lock was achieved, the object reacted by changing its shape to a triangle and increasing its speed to over 620 miles an hour. The onboard radar tapes of the F-16s show that the UFO descended from six thousand feet to just under three thousand feet in two seconds. This represents a G-force of 45, which is more than the human body or any man-made machine can withstand. The object then moved in a zigzag pattern over the city of Brussels, as if taking evasive action so the fighters could not get a missile lock on them.

Like its counterpart in the Hudson Valley of New York, the UFO in Belgium was seen by thousands of witnesses and tracked on radar by ground-to-air and air-to-air systems. Although sightings have died down since that time, the UFO is still being seen. From the information that I obtained recently, the number of cases of contact and abductions there have increased considerably. This was also true in the Hudson Valley, and it is an important fact to remember. It seems that the UFOs would do an initial scanning of an area to locate people who are compatible for their purpose and to locate others that they "tagged" as a child. I will never forget the words of veteran researcher and author Budd Hopkins when I asked why he thought there were so many sightings concentrated in small areas for a length of time. Budd replied, "Because they are looking for people." When he first said this to me in 1985, I didn't think too much of it, but now I believe his statement was the answer to my question.

In the fall of 1990, I gave a presentation about the Belgium UFO sightings at the Omega UFO Conference in North Haven, Connecticut. Although I felt a little uneasy since I did not personally investigate the sightings until 1992, I had a great deal of data on the case, which was sent to me by the original researchers. The presentation turned out very well, and I was able to answer all the questions asked by the audience of over three hundred people.

FOUR

EXTRATERRESTRIAL
UFOS

If you have read a great deal of material concerning the UFO phenomenon or have personally investigated sightings on your own, you may have come to the realization that our planet Earth is a very strange place with many unsolved mysteries. According to a recent Gallup poll, there are growing numbers of people who are convinced that such things as poltergeists, psychic phenomena, and UFOs are more than the overactive imagination of a bored society. As researchers, our investigations concerning unexplained phenomena so far has been restricted to the surface of our planet. However, with the recent boom in technology it is now possible to expand the senses of a human being to such a great extent that the invisible universe is now coming into focus. The scientific instruments of the twenty-first century are available to anyone, and they are amazing indeed, so amazing that just fifty years ago such technology would have been considered science fiction.

With the awareness of the human mind greatly enhanced through instrumentation, we are now able to monitor not only the space around us, but also the entire solar system. With every mystery we solve, ten new ones arise, and we see that the universe has an astronomical number of unexplained events to keep researchers and scientists busy for many years. Some of these occurrences are so far beyond our current understanding that many people want to attach supernatural or religious significance to them. It must be pointed out that scientists of the eighteenth century tried in vain to explain how our sun could produce so much energy over such a long period of time. In the eighteenth century, nuclear fusion was unknown and the power source of the sun remained a mystery until the twentieth century. Today we are faced with the same problem; we just do not have the understanding and technology to explain all the paranormal events that we observe.

When we cannot explain something we experience, some will claim it just does not exist because it does not fit in with current theory, while others will claim it was an act of God and meant for us not to understand. This is the case with the UFO phenomenon, and it is mainly because of our limited understanding of the cosmos. On one hand, science has ignored the reports because they do not fit into current theory, while on the other hand, others claim they represent manifestations of supernatural beings.

Human beings continue to make the same mistakes over and over; this is evident in history. The scientists who profess knowledge to our younger generation today are guilty of the same mistakes as their predecessors of the seventeenth century. One of these mistakes is the attitude that "if we can't explain it, it must not be real." As part of a prerequisite for graduation, all prospective scientists should read one of the many versions of the trial of Galileo. The intellectuals of his day refused to look through his telescope because they said what he claimed just could not exist. Today, of course, we know that the observations of Galileo set the foundations for modern astronomy. However, after the trial of Galileo, it took almost one hundred years for his ideas to be accepted. Galileo was considered to be a heretic in his day, yet he opened a door to new worlds that were unimaginable for his time.

Having been a science educator for the past twenty-seven years, I see the same thing taking place right now in the twenty-first century. Do we dare repeat the same mistakes? I feel it is very wrong to say that a paranormal phenomenon does not exist just because it doesn't fit within the confines of our understanding of the universe. It is also incorrect to label these occurrences as being occult, supernatural, or an act of God. The late Dr. J. Allen Hynek, in my opinion, was a modern-day Galileo. When asked about his opinion of what are called the borderline sciences, he said, "I believe that paranormal phenomena, especially UFOs, is the science of the twenty-second century."

Dr. Hynek believed that a study of UFOs could actually yield more information about the true state of the cosmos than our entire space program has over the past thirty years. Not only is it very important to study these paranormal events on our planet, but also to try to document them outside Earth, since if they are taking place here, then the same events should be taking place in other parts of the universe. Perhaps it will give us a much broader understanding of UFOs and related phenomena. Documentation of UFO activity in the space around our planet has already begun by a small number of researchers, of which I happen to be one.

MISSING SPACE PROBES

The late, great rocket scientist Dr. Hermann Oberth was so intrigued by the UFO phenomenon that he collected reports for years, but kept this interest so secret that many of his colleagues had no idea that he was doing UFO research. In a 1954 news conference, Oberth told reporters that the evidence of UFOs or flying saucers indicates that they may be spaceships of some kind piloted by interplanetary beings. Dr. Oberth speculated that the UFOs may use the moon and the planet Mars as a base to get to Earth. He was also sure that when the time comes to explore the solar system, this intelligence may have something to say about it and interfere with our missions to the moon and especially our exploration of Mars.

Since the era of the exploration of Mars began in the early 1960s, over half of Earth's unmanned probes sent to the planet have failed, and many of them just disappeared. In 1993, NASA lost communication with a probe just as it was ready to go into orbit. This incident was of great concern to NASA, since a few years earlier several Russian Martian probes also met with the same fate. According to the Russian government, a large, cylindrical object was detected intercepting the Soviet Phobos 2 spacecraft before it vanished. It could be that whoever is out there may want us to see only what they think we should. There have also been a good number of cases involving missing satellites, and documentation of Soviet and American astronauts having UFO sightings while in space.

ASTRONAUTS AND UFOS

Since the early sixties, the people of planet Earth have sent astronauts and cosmonauts into the space around our planet. Did any of these early missions into space ever witness a UFO? The answer to that question is yes, they did, but you rarely heard about it through the media. The American astronauts who had sightings of unknown objects in space include Gordon Cooper, Ed White, James McDivitt, James Lovell, Frank Borman, Buzz Aldrin, Donald Slayton, Pete Conrad, Scott Carpenter, Michael Collins, and the first man to walk on the moon, Neil Armstrong.

Gordon Cooper, who was one of the original Mercury astronauts, orbited Earth twenty-two times on May 15, 1963, and was the last American to fly alone in space. During his final orbit, he told the tracking station that he saw a greenish, glowing object ahead of him approaching his capsule. The UFO was also picked up by the tracking station and, according to their data, it was a solid object of considerable size. The sighting was covered by the major television networks at the time, but the media was not allowed to talk to astronaut Cooper. After he left active duty, Gordon Cooper became a firm believer in the reality of UFOs. Cooper on a number of occasions has made public statements to the effect that the

Figure 6. UFO imaged by Gemini IX mission, 1965.

government is withholding information about flying saucers from the American public.

In June of 1965, astronauts Ed White and James McDivitt were passing over Hawaii in the Gemini spacecraft when they saw a metallic-like object in the distance (fig. 6, object reported by Gemini IX). The UFO had long arm-like extensions sticking out of its body, as if they were used to grab objects in space. McDivitt took a number of pictures that were never released to the American public.

In December of 1965, Gemini 7 astronauts James Lovell and Frank Borman also had a UFO sighting while in Earth orbit. Borman reported an unidentified object some distance from their capsule. Gemini control at Cape Kennedy told him that he was seeing the booster from the final stage of their own Titan rocket. Borman confirmed that he saw the booster, but there was something else next to it. Gemini control could not verify that a second object was there—it was invisible to their tracking equipment.

Neil Armstrong, the first man to walk on the moon, has gone on record by saying he believed in UFOs. According to a number of unconfirmed reports, both Armstrong and Buzz Aldrin saw UFOs after they landed on the lunar surface on July 21, 1969. The only official conformation that we do have about the sighting is while they were broadcasting the lunar landing live to the world command module, Michael Collins, in lunar orbit, made an announcement that he saw a strange light in one of the craters of the moon. He asked for more information, and then the audio to the command module went dead. It seemed that Mission Control went to a private channel and took his audio off the live worldwide television broadcast. According to former NASA employees, the conversation was still picked up by ham radio operators who were lucky enough to find the secret VHF frequency. These operators claim that the astronauts reported seeing a giant alien spacecraft at the edge of a crater just sitting there as if watching them.

WHAT ABOUT THOSE
STRANGE LUNAR LIGHTS?

The moon is our closest neighbor in space and one of the most frequently observed celestial objects by amateur and professional astronomers alike. There have been reports of strange lights on the surface of the moon for hundreds of years. Astronomers have reported seeing balls of light flying across the lunar surface or emerging from the dark floors of many craters.

The lunar lights have been explained away as static electricity on the moon, gases emitting from ancient lunar volcanoes, and plasma from solar flares getting trapped on the lunar surface. The truth of this matter is that science cannot explain the lunar lights, so they were all labeled as "transient lunar phenomena" or TLP. To the astronomer, any kind of unusual short-lived activity or event on the moon is now classified as a TLP. Types of TLP that have been reported over the years include red glows and flashes in craters, abnormal reflections, and balls of light that seem to fly across the lunar surface under intelligent control. Some "experts" are inclined to dismiss TLP as either aberrational effects in our atmosphere or illusions created by the changing illumination of the moon.

Accounts of TLP date back to the time of William Herschel who, in 1781, discovered the planet Uranus. Herschel reported in his journal that on a number of occasions, while observing the moon with his telescope, he witnessed strange globes of lights jump from crater to crater. This proved to Herschel that there was life on the moon, but the astronomers of his day did not accept his theories and soon they were forgotten. In 1958, Soviet astronomer Nikolai Kozyrev saw a red glowing light in the lunar crater Alphonsus. He reported that an analysis of the light indicated the presence of the element carbon, the building block for life.

TLP: FROM BIRDS TO UFOS

About ten years ago, I was sent a video of the full moon taken by a Japanese amateur astronomer that showed strange balls of light apparently moving across the lunar surface. The spheres were moving so fast that they traversed the entire diameter of the moon in a matter of seconds. The video was shown all over the Nippon Network in Japan, and the fellow who took the video was on all the major talk shows in that country. A copy of the video was sent to me for my comments and analysis. When I played the video, I was surprised to see these objects streak so fast across the moon that it was almost impossible get a good look at them. So I slowed down the video and froze each frame and enlarged the image. To my surprise, they didn't look like globes of light at all. One of the "balls" was clear enough so that I could make it out: what was videotaped were actually birds flying across the full moon.

I have seen this before while looking at the bright full moon, birds that are flying between the moon and the telescope can actually be seen by the eye. Since these birds were white, they reflected the bright lunar light and due to the magnification of the telescope they appear to streak by at great speed. This made the birds appear as spheres on the low resolution video tape. When I enlarged the image further and played it in slow motion, I could actually see a hint of flapping wings. Some mysteries can be solved if we look long enough and use common sense, but many cannot.

The best example of TLP that I have ever seen was taken in Connecticut by an amateur astronomer who photographed

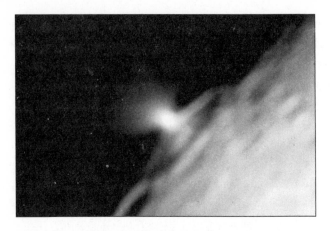

Figure 7. Strange lights on the moon.

Figure 8. Notice how the light moved and got brighter.

a strange brilliant light moving across the lunar surface. The light then hovered above a crater, illuminating the crater floor, moved to the right, and, with a burst of energy, shot off into space (fig. 7 and fig. 8). The image was analyzed by a number of experts (including myself) in the fields of photography and astronomy and found to be a large light source moving across the lunar surface and not any type of optical illusion. Are these strange lunar lights proof of alien spacecraft on our nearest neighbor in space, or are they something more exotic, like actual living beings or space creatures that can exist in the cold vacuum of space? This idea will be explored later as I present material that is not normally found in a book about UFOs, but has a definite connection and importance to our understanding of the phenomenon.

SOMEONE IS TAMPERING WITH OUR SATELLITES

If you saw the movie *Independence Day*, you will remember the scene in which a strange beeping tone was received on Earth-based satellite equipment. This beeping was a relayed communication from an alien mothership that was using our satellites to communicate with its warships stationed across the world over every major city. Although the movie was a combination of science fiction and fantasy, some of the things presented are in fact true. There really is an Area 51, and yes, the United States and European governments have known for years that someone out there is tampering with our satellites and space probes. For decades the governments of the world have imaged unknown objects in space approaching our satellites in Earth orbit. They also have received strange transmissions similar to Morse code, which seem to be coming from a point beyond the moon and bounced off our satellites to some unknown location on Earth. Is some alien intelligence using our satellites and if so, for what purpose?

In 1976, the Lamont-Doherty Earth Observatory, located in Palisades, New York, picked up a strange coded signal on a narrow frequency band. The story was so bizarre that it was carried in a number of major newspapers in New Jersey and New York. What was strange was that the signal was picked up on most of their equipment, indicating that it had no point of origin on this planet. These signals were received the same time that UFOs were being seen within a ten-mile radius of the observatory. It was found that the signals did not come from Earth, but somewhere in space in a straight line from where the UFOs were seen. Was some unknown intelligence sending instructions to their craft over the skies of New Jersey?

Not only have strange signals and images been recorded in the memory banks of the computers that operate our satellites, but our satellites in space have also vanished for no apparent reason. Each orbiting space vehicle is equipped with a radio transmitter that sends out a signal on a number of frequencies. These signals not only transmit valuable information to the operators on the surface, but they also transmit a coded ID identifying the satellite. There are several types of satellites now in orbit and the actual number is somewhere around five thousand. Most of these satellites are communication satellites, while the rest of them are scientific and military.

Those of you who have read my first two books, *Night Siege: The Hudson Valley UFO Sightings* and *Contact of the 5th Kind*, know that in the past, in somewhat of a limited way, I was involved with military intelligence during the Vietnam War. Although I have had no official connection with such operations since 1973, there are people whom I was very close to at the time that actually stayed in the military and today have very influential positions in the CIA. Because of these past connections, I have been privileged to information regarding military involvement with UFOs.

In 1996, I was introduced to a radar operator who was stationed at the NORAD complex in Boulder, Colorado. NORAD tracks all objects in the space around Earth and is responsible for the early-warning system in the event of a nuclear attack upon the United States. This individual told me that on a number of occasions, objects were seen approaching our satellites as if checking them out and then moved away. In rare cases, these objects also merged with the satellite on the screen and, as the object moved away, our satellite simply was not there anymore, and its radio tracking signal vanished.

This person also told me that on many occasions, objects were seen moving to and away from Earth at incredible speeds. They are classified as top secret and are referred to using the code name "Fast Walker." I found this statement very interesting, and some time later I was informed that noted UFO researcher Jacque Vallee published a book with a similar title. I do know from my own experiences with tracking satellites that several of them have vanished. Such was the case of NOAA 13, which vanished in 1995. The Chinese have also lost two satellites, Feyung I and II. The Russians have lost a total of three that I know of, and again they just vanished. None of these spacecrafts burned up in the atmosphere or got lost in space—they simply vanished.

SATELLITE IMAGES OF UFOS

I had heard from a number of different sources that images of UFOs in space had been picked up by satellites in both geostationary and polar orbit. I decided to investigate the matter in greater detail. I was able to obtain designs of a home satellite-reception station given to me by a computer and mechanical engineer in California, so I modified his plans and built a system that receives and images transmissions directly from satellites in orbit around Earth. This system uses a common VHF receiver that has been modified to a narrow bandwidth, a decoder-demodulator system with the proper software, and finally a personal computer. The antennas that are used are of two types. The first is a standard omnidirectional to pick up the polar orbiting satellites and the other is a dish with a diameter of about one meter for those satellites in geostationary orbit.

For the most part, the majority of satellite transmissions are encrypted and just about impossible to image (but it has been done). The easiest satellites to receive on your home computer are the ones with scientific designation. Of these scientific satellites, the meteorological ones are a good choice because they transmit on common frequencies and are easy to decode. In fact, most people do not know that hundreds of images of Earth and the space around our planet are transmitted from these satellites to ground receiving stations each day. With a modest investment, it is possible to obtain these images from at least ten different satellites that belong to the United States, Russia, Japan, and Europe. Many generations of these satellites have been in use for years, and occasionally they image something strange in the space surrounding our planet. For decades these images went unnoticed by the public, until people in a number of different countries began to access them.

Since 1991, I have been receiving images of our planet and the space around it, searching each frame for something unusual. The "Earth station" that I built at this time was a prototype system upon which many other scientific researchers would later base their designs. My work in this area was published in a scientific journal called *Earth* (May 1992) and resulted in many calls from universities, experimental researchers, and finally the United Nations. It was also selected as one of the ten best articles in a scientific journal, and it appeared in a number of university publications as a research guide. From those early days of satellite reception until the present, I received and saved thousands of images but only twelve were of something that could be classified as a true anomaly, in other words a UFO. It is not possible to present all of these images in this book, but I will cover the most interesting of them. I must make it clear, however, that my primary intention for designing and building this receiver was not looking for UFOs; it was a research project for my school to give students a better understanding of our planet.

STRANGE IMAGES IN SPACE

The geostationary satellites are in a fixed position as seen from the surface of Earth at an altitude of about 24,800 miles, while the polar orbiting satellites circle our planet at an altitude from 400 to 1,200 miles. Their north–south paths around our planet are designed to pass directly over an area once a day, which means they make one complete circle around Earth about every 70 to 90 minutes. Each successive orbit will find them passing more to the west from any location on the surface of Earth. Both types of satellites use very little transmitting power (less than 5 watts, which is about the power of a night-light in your home). But despite this low power, with the right equipment you can receive a clear, sharp image of planet Earth from space.

THE IMAGE THAT STARTED IT ALL

The first time I received something unusual was on October 24, 1994 (yes, three years after I put the system together). The satellite imaged was called NOAA 12, a polar orbiting satellite at an altitude of about 500 miles. NOAA 12 circles the Earth at a speed of 10,000 miles an hour and was passing over the Atlantic Ocean between Africa and Brazil. The image was in the infrared and one could clearly see the temperature difference between the air and ocean currents. On the image was a triangular object, which was too perfect in geometric shape to have been a bizarre flaw in the imaging system. Whatever it was, it was huge and passed directly under the satellite, blocking out a section of the surface of the earth. As

I studied the image, a chill went up and down my spine. Here was an object of triangular shape, a shape that I have become very familiar with, because over the past twenty-plus years I have been investigating the appearance of a similar object in New York's Hudson River Valley. As I continued to study the image, I wondered how large it really was. Judging by the darkness of its color, it was giving off a considerable amount of heat. I decided at that time just to put the image aside, and I began monitoring the system more closely to see what else might come in. This was not an easy thing to do since I can receive more than a hundred images over a twenty-four-hour period. However, the next strange image of something unknown would not come in until November 3, 1994.

On November 3 at about 9:00 a.m. (EST), I was monitoring the equipment and already had gone through sixty-five files of stored satellite images from around the world captured that night. As I watched the screen, the familiar beeping sound of a United States NOAA polar orbiter began to come in on the receiver. I quickly turned to the computer, and the satellite-tracking program identified it as belonging to NOAA 12, a satellite that travels from north to south (this is the same satellite that imaged the anomaly in October).

As the image came in on the computer screen at the usual rate of 120 lines per minute, it was clear that it had once again captured something highly unusual. On the screen were two triangular-shaped objects that were very close to the satellite. NOAA 12 at this time was passing between the tip of Florida and South America. Once again the image was obtained in the infrared by a method called APT (automatic picture transmission), a real-time image of that section of planet Earth as seen from space. Again, the objects appeared jet-black, indicating that they were very hot. Perhaps they were moving as fast as the satellite and the friction of our atmosphere was causing them to give out large amounts of heat. I switched to the normal visible light and the objects were barely visible—I really had to look hard to see them. UFOs radiate in the infrared, and this may be one of the reasons why we do not see them more frequently with our eyes.

Since the objects were very geometric and did not appear on a regular basis, I was sure that they were not some type of imaging flaw in the satellite or my computer program. I could make out the basic shape of the objects, but to see further detail was impossible, since I was dealing with two-dimensional images. The objects were most likely very large, since from my estimates they were at least several miles below the satellite and moving at about the same speed.

I then showed the two pictures to an associate of mine who is a scientist with a strong background in the designing of satellite-imaging systems. He agreed that the shapes were strange and not consistent with what is commonly called "missing data." I have seen many forms of missing data, and it seems to be a common occurrence with the polar orbiting satellites, but these shapes were something totally different. The data was in fact missing, but something was under the satellite imaging system blocking it out! My associate, being a conservative scientist, then told me that he would require a great deal more data before he could be convinced that they were UFOs in orbit around our planet. He said, "It would be nice if you could image something in space near Earth that is more spherical in shape, then the image could be studied in greater detail." I agreed, but I felt that the chances of getting something like that were very remote, because the two images obtained so far were the result of years of work and thousands of files.

THE IMAGE I HAD HOPED FOR

Nothing unusual was picked up for quite some time, and for the most part I would leave the system on automatic and then check the files when the hard drive would get too full. Each image takes up a quarter of a megabyte of disk space, and I could receive as many as one hundred images in a twenty-four-hour period. On March 15, 1995, I went through the images as I do each morning, and after fifty files I started to become discouraged. I almost began to erase the entire series of files when I had a feeling to just check a few more.

The next file showed an infrared image of North America from the GOES 8 satellite. The image was taken on March 14, 1995, at 14:45 GMT. The channel used was number 4, which meant it was measuring the temperature of the cloud cover. One could easily see a major storm brewing in the southwest. In the upper left of the frame in space was a glowing disk-like object that was very hot in the infrared (fig. 9, satellite image of UFO from GOES 8). This object looked black in relation to the clear, cold space around it. The system had picked up its first disk. The object was moving out of the frame, and when the next image came into the same area twenty-five minutes later, the UFO was no longer there! I then color-enhanced the

Figure 9. Image of unknown disk-shaped
object near Earth imaged by GOES 8.

image, and it showed something interesting. As I got farther
from the disk, the colors would change from very hot ones to
cooler ones. This is what one would expect if the UFO were
radiating heat, since the farther one would move from the
heat source, the cooler the space around it would get.

I showed the image to a number of people involved in the
technical and scientific fields, and everyone seemed quite
amazed. My friend who was the satellite-imaging specialist
said the picture was "interesting" and proposed a theory that
it was a freak image of the moon, and for some reason the
satellite identified it incorrectly and darkened it. I asked him
if he had ever seen the moon in the situation he described,
and his answer was a quick *NO!* Our moon is not an infrared
source—I have seen the moon before in satellite images, and
it is barely visible. Furthermore, the UFO was much too high

on the celestial sphere to be our natural satellite, and then twenty-five minutes later, it was gone.

This image put renewed energy into my task, and I was now convinced that UFOs were orbiting our planet and darting in and out of our atmosphere. At that time, I was accessing a small number of satellites with low to moderate resolution capabilities, and I wondered what the government had in their possession and how long they were keeping a record of these outer-space close encounters.

A COSMIC JOKE?

The next image of a UFO was to be the most perplexing to date. On the morning of June 8, 1995, at 11:45 GMT, I was sitting at the console of the station, watching an image slowly being formed on the screen. I was quite surprised to see a disk-like object in the lower screen near the southern part of the Pacific Ocean. Whatever it was, it looked like the classic disk-shaped UFO and it seemed to have multiple layers or portals of some sort (fig. 10). I thought at first that someone was playing some type of cosmic joke on me, but then I realized that this was a real, solid object hovering several thousand miles above the surface of Earth. Again, the image was in the infrared from the GOES 8 satellite, but this time using imaging channel number 3. This object must have been a great deal closer to the satellite since the resolution was much better than I was able to obtain in previous pictures.

I decided to send a copy of the image to NOAA (National Oceanic Atmospheric Administration). Several days later, I was contacted by an imaging scientist by phone whose official

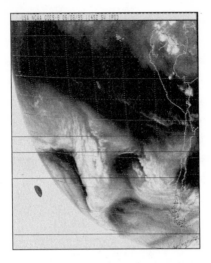

Figure 10. Image of disk-shaped
UFO with layers by GOES 8.

title was "Director of Analyzing Anomalies." I thought that
the title was strange, since the government officially stated
that these objects do not exist. Yet they had someone on their
staff whose job was to analyze images like the one obtained
from orbiting satellites. This could only mean one thing, and
that was that they have received UFO images and are very
interested in them. NOAA had no knowledge of the June 8
image and had to go into their files to find it. They said that
they were very perplexed as to what the image was, and the
lines on the object were something they could not explain.
I continued a dialog with NOAA for several months on this
matter, but then they suddenly would not comment anymore
on the image.

The image was also sent to NASA and the Jet Propulsion Laboratory (JPL) in Pasadena, California. Although JPL would not comment on the image, NASA did. It was their opinion that the image is an unknown anomaly. This was a cautious way of saying that they didn't know what the hell it was. I also showed them the other images that I had obtained, and they said they were nothing more than "moon shadows." When I asked them to explain just what a moon shadow was, I was told that because the moon is so bright in the sky, it is reflected off the satellite's imaging system, producing a dark object. Because of this, the computer imaging system onboard the satellite mistakenly identifies it as a heat source. I also asked them if they have seen this often and was told no, that this was never brought to their attention before. When selecting images for weather forecasting, the computers at NOAA and NASA will often reject images that have an anomaly in them since it could mean a flaw with those WEFAX (weatherfax) images, and they are ignored.

A CYLINDRICAL–SHAPED UFO
WITH MARKINGS

Another interesting image was obtained by my Earth station on June 4, 1998, from the polar orbiting satellite NOAA 14 (fig. 11, satellite NOAA 14 image of UFO). The image showed the Atlantic Ocean with nearby Central America and a number of weather formations including a severe thunderstorm off the coast of Costa Rica. In the upper left-hand portion of the image was a solid, metallic-looking cylindrical object with markings on it. I thought at first that it was just space junk, but no

Figure 11. Image of cylindrical object below
the NOAA 14 polar orbiting satellite.

NOAA satellite has ever imaged space junk, since the satellite would be moving much too fast for the image to process.
This object was well below NOAA 14 and moving at the same
speed as the satellite. The object clearly had fins and was moving from north to south. Once again the image is unexplainable and gives validation that the space around our planet is
very active with UFO activity.

Not only do the CIA and NASA store images from satellites, but so does the University of Colorado. Most of these
images are stored automatically and never looked at by a
real person. Somehow, some way, scientists at Colorado got
wind of the images that were picked up on my satellite reception system and they went digging into their own files.
During April of 2001, I received an anonymous letter from

an individual who claimed he was a member of the University of Colorado's meteorology team. The following is an abridged version of that letter.

Mr. Imbrogno,

The image that you have obtained . . . was picked up by the GOES satellite—from what I know about this system and [the method that it uses to obtain] data, [it] is definitely not the moon. I refer to the GOES 8 image from June 8, 1995, at 11:45 Zulu. Your research into this area has made me go into our files to find that particular image, and when I did, I almost fell out of the chair I was sitting in, since I have seen that image before from another satellite. NASA, the CIA, and other agencies review thousands of satellite images a day. This was the same image that was sent to our team in 1995 from the CIA asking to identify the object if we could. We analyzed the image with every method possible and did days of computer calculations, which included the position of the moon. Our result was that the image *is not the moon* or a flaw in the computer system on GOES 8. It was labeled as an "anomaly" by the chief of our team and sent back to the CIA. Two days later, our director received a call from the CIA telling us that the image and all data is an issue of national security and is now labeled as "classified secret." We were all told not to say anything about this, so you can see why I was so surprised when I saw a copy of the same image we were told to be quiet about. We have dozens of images taken of the moon from all the GOES satellites in the infrared and visible light, and you can barely see it in the background. This image that you have is not the moon nor can it not be explained as a flaw or other computer glitch. I am writing this letter since I have retired and I want people to know that the government does hide things about UFOs and they put considerable pressure on the scientific community to cooperate with them in these matters. I hope someday you will write another book and publish this letter. In the meantime, I intend to pick up your book *Night Siege: The Hudson Valley UFO Sightings* to get a better understanding of this entire UFO situation. You have permission to use any part of this letter for your research, and I wish you the best in making the public aware that these things called UFOs are very real!

Sincerely,
Anonymous

After I read this letter, it encouraged me to continue to collect images, so I modified the system to make it more sensitive and to obtain sharper images, especially in the infrared and the channels that obtain water vapor readings in the atmosphere. Every morning I would check the images for the past twenty-four hours, and to my surprise, one morning when I went through them, many of the images were blacked out. Instead of a nice, clear picture of our planet in space, there was a fax data sheet that said, "Product not available on WEFAX." Since that time, although I am still able to get

GOES 8, 9, and 10 images, at least 10 percent of them are blacked out! Also, as of the writing of this book, I have not obtained any more images of unusual objects from the GOES system.

Is someone now monitoring the images more closely and censoring the UFO images? It is possible that some government agency is watching the images very carefully now, and anything that looks strange is blacked out so that people like me cannot get them. I became quite frustrated, since I felt I was on to something important, and I kicked myself for releasing the information too soon. I should have just secretly imaged the satellites for years until I collected enough data, so that no one in the government could explain it all away as a "moon shadow."

SETTING UP YOUR OWN EARTH STATION

Today any PC will do the job of imaging satellite transmissions. The computer should have a com port in the back, since this is how the demodulator feeds the signal into the computer for decoding. However, with the proper adapter, a USB port will also work. Environmental satellites transmit on the frequencies between 136 and 138 MHz in the 2-meter band. A receiver that works well for this purpose is a programmable "police" scanner or an amateur radio receiver that has these frequencies in the FM band. A stock receiver will work; however, the bandwidth should be adjusted to be between 30 and 50 kHz. This makes the receiver's ability to receive wide enough to obtain all the information in the transmission. If you just want to listen in on the satellites as they orbit our planet, then all you need is the scanner receiver and any length of copper wire to act as an antenna. As the satellite passes overhead, you will hear a beeping sound. It is possible to receive the transmission from as far north as Canada and as far south as Brazil. The best frequencies to use are 137.50, 137.620, 137.30, 137.40, and 137.850. You should not restrict yourself to these frequencies, since other signals have been picked up outside this range. These are the frequencies allowed for American, Chinese, European, and Russian satellites of the polar orbiting type, and their transmissions can be received as they move above your horizon.

THE ANTENNA

As previously stated, a length of thick copper wire will do, but there are antennas specifically designed for satellite reception. Many types of antennas for the 2-meter band can be purchased at stores like RadioShack. I once used a Yagi TV antenna and got very clear reception of transmissions from satellites like NOAA and Meteor polar orbiting spacecraft. You should connect the receiver with the antenna with RG59/U cable, which is your typical cable-TV wire.

GOES RECEPTION

To receive the GOES transmissions, you will need a down converter, a small dish antenna, plus the equipment mentioned previously. It's not as complex or expensive as it sounds. You could put together a very good Earth station for under two thousand dollars, not counting the computer. If any of my readers would like further information, plus detailed instructions on setting up your own satellite-receiving station, please contact me at the address or e-mail located in the appendix of this book. If you have your own station, I would like to keep in contact with you and possibly set up a network to watch the celestial sphere around our planet.

FIVE

A MULTITUDE
OF DIMENSIONS

When human beings are confronted with something they do not understand, they normally refuse to believe it and will look for reasons not to accept something that has jeopardized the security that they have built around them. The majority of people on this planet are also Earth chauvinists, which means they want to believe that this world and society of ours is the ultimate place for intelligence in the universe. People have made this mistake for many generations and have even used religion to establish this claim.

At one time the great thinkers of the middle ages claimed that our Earth was the center of the universe. It was a shock to the ego of humanity when it was finally discovered that our little planet really didn't have a special place in the solar system. Then, in the nineteenth century, it was discovered that our sun is but one of billions of stars in an island universe that came to be known as the Milky Way galaxy. The great thinkers of the day insisted that our sun was in the center of the galaxy; their argument was that since we were made in the image of God, human beings had to have a special place in creation. This idea did not last very long, and a short time later, at the beginning of the twentieth century, we found out that we were not in the center of the galaxy, but in a little obscure place located thirty thousand light years from the center in a spiral arm, out in the boondocks of our island universe. This would once again have a devastating effect on the ego of human beings on planet Earth—to discover that we were not located in any special place in God's creation. However, it didn't stop there.

By the early to mid-twentieth century, other galaxies besides our own were discovered and scientists were shocked to learn that our Milky Way is but one of millions of galaxies that surround us in the visible universe. By observing the location of these galaxies on the celestial sphere, it appeared as if they were evenly distributed around us. This made it seem that our galaxy was the center of the universe; however, once again, by the end of the twentieth century, earthlings were to find that this was not the case—our galaxy held no special place in the cosmos. Today, in the twenty-first century, we see that our ideas were wrong about the universe, and scientists are now very cautious when they once again try to put our tiny planet in the center of all and everything. You would think that at this point the people of Earth would learn from their past mistakes, but they do not. Each generation seems to repeat the same mistakes that their parents, teachers, and leaders did, and their attitude toward the UFO phenomenon is no exception.

WINDOWS IN TIME AND SPACE

A mistake that many paranormal researchers have made in the past and continue to make today is that they try to label the entire UFO experience with one explanation. There are quite a number of groups that have different beliefs for the origins of UFOs, but all of them seem too locked into one idea to explain the phenomenon. The UFO experience is very complex and most likely has a multitude of origins. We are in fact viewing and experiencing a number of different types of phenomena and giving it one label to make it easier to understand.

In the final years of his life, Dr. Hynek no longer believed in the extraterrestrial theory for the origin of UFOs. We had many conversations about the subject, and he expressed his doubts that UFOs were physical craft from other star systems. To quote Dr. Hynek, "I have come to support less and less the idea that UFOs are nuts-and-bolts spacecrafts from other worlds. There are just too many things that go against that theory. To me, it seems ridiculous that a technologically advanced race would travel great distances to do relatively stupid things like stop cars, collect soil samples, and frighten people. I think we must begin to re-examine the evidence; we must look closer to home for the answer. I think we should consider that UFOs come from other dimensions, a parallel reality, a universe that exists in the same place as ours, but at a different frequency, so to speak."

Hynek also started to see the connection between UFO reports and certain types of psychic phenomena, because there are many UFO cases that have poltergeists, apparitions, strange sounds and lights, and other types of psychic manifestations attached to them. Over the many years that I have been researching the phenomenon, I have found this to be true. Quite a number of UFO case studies are like ghost stories rather than encounters with spaceships and beings from another star system.

Just before Allen Hynek passed over, he told me that he believed that there were windows in time and space that opened up periodically and bridged one parallel reality with another. He believed that when this took place it was possible for beings in that world to come into ours and for us to go into theirs. Dr. Hynek and I discussed the locations of the "windows" as he called them, and theorized that the portals or windows most likely take place where UFOs are seen frequently and in great numbers. One of these locations was right in my backyard, the Hudson River Valley. Allen Hynek then challenged me to try and find the locations of these interdimensional "windows." This led me into another direction that connected the UFO phenomenon with an ancient people whose understanding of a multidimensional universe was common knowledge to them and an important part of their religion.

WINDOWS IN MY BACKYARD

I firmly believe that Dr. Hynek's theory about interdimensional "windows" was somehow connected with the UFO phenomenon. If many of the sightings are the result of some type of dimensional vehicle or even a life form, then they must enter our reality through some type of portal, something similar to a natural or artificially created wormhole. At that time, I had quite a number of sightings logged into my computer—nearly seven thousand were collected in the past ten years. I took the UFO and paranormal reports in the Hudson Valley, nearby Connecticut, New Jersey, and Massachusetts; started to classify them according to the type of encounter; and plotted them on two very large wall maps of that area of the northeast. I found that the UFO sightings fell into two categories. The first were the general sightings, that is, witnesses who saw a UFO at an altitude of one thousand feet or higher, in other words just a sighting. The second were the cases of "high strangeness," or those of the close encounter and contact type. I also included paranormal and psychic phenomena that were reported on or near the time and date of the UFO sighting.

When the first map was completed, it really showed no distinct pattern. It seemed that the UFO was being reported in the entire tri-state area of Connecticut, New York, and New Jersey. I even included about a dozen sightings from southern Massachusetts, which according to reports was an object of similar description to that which was being spotted in the Hudson River Valley of New York. There was one interesting thing that I did notice on the map—the center or the focus of all the UFO activity seemed to be in Putnam County, New York, between the towns of Kent Cliffs, Putnam Valley, and Carmel. The UFO seemed to make its first and last appearance in these locations. There was no doubt about the accuracy of the plotted data, since the majority of the reports were made by high caliber witnesses. I then asked myself, was this the location of one of Allen Hynek's "windows"?

When the second map was completed, it surprised me because it showed that the high strangeness reports were clustered around the towns of Kent Cliffs, Putnam Valley, and nearby Southeast, New York. These clusters or hot spots of paranormal activity were no larger than a quarter of a mile in diameter, and the locations were not random, they were in fact arranged in straight lines! The next thing I planned on doing was to go out and visit some of these locations and see what I could find.

This was not as easy as it sounds, since in many cases I had to survey an entire area, trek through heavy brush, and walk miles into the backcountry where only hunters and hikers go. This took quite a bit of time and many of these locations still remain unexplored. I enlisted the aid of a number of people who, in the past, volunteered their time to help me investigate UFO and paranormal reports in the area. While journeying out to these locations, we used 10-meter amateur radios to help our "away" teams keep in touch with the field base. For some reason, which was unknown to me at the time, I had trouble establishing communication with teams just a mile away. Since we were transmitting with quite a great deal of power (ten times what would be used in normal radio communication), there was no reason why we should not have been able to maintain radio contact with the other teams. We did receive a great deal of static and strange interference that sounded like it was being generated by a high-frequency coil. Because of this problem, we switched our communication equipment to 2-meter FM. This seemed to work much better, and we got less static and much greater range. I found out that the interference generated strongly on the 8- to 20-meter band in the AM and the upper and lower sidebands, and it was so strong that it jammed radio communications on these frequencies, making radio contact very difficult, if not impossible.

MYSTERIOUS MEGALITHS

One of the things that my exploration teams discovered was that in just about every location we surveyed, there was a strange carved standing stone or a stone chamber close to the center of the reported paranormal activity (fig. 12, the "Balanced Rock" in North Salem, New York). At first I thought that this was a coincidence, but when these stone structures kept on showing up, I realized that whoever built these things placed them at these locations for a reason. I also found that the greatest numbers of these stone chambers are in the Putnam Valley/Kent Cliffs area of Putnam County, New York, the same locations as the center or apex of the UFO activity.

Figure 12. The "Balanced Rock"
in North Salem, New York.

Figure 13. Stone chamber and standing
stone located in Holmes, New York.

The stone chambers of the Hudson Valley are an enigma. No one knows who built them or how long ago (fig. 13, stone chamber with standing stone). My research has shown that the chambers may have been built by Celtic explorers with the help of a number of Druid priests thousands of years ago. The Druids believed in a parallel universe, or worlds of spirits, and this could be why these structures were built in these areas, perhaps to mark the location of a window.

Many sites in Ireland and Scotland that are hot spots for UFOs, paranormal phenomena, and crop circles are located on what was once Druid sacred ground. These areas were also always marked by standing stones or other megalithic structures. The stone chambers and standing stones in New York are identical to the megalithic structures of the British Isles, and it seems that a very ancient people came to the northeast

United States a very long time ago and marked the sacred areas (locations of the windows) with a chamber (temple) or a carved standing stone. My work in this area is documented in my book *Celtic Mysteries: Windows to Another Dimension in America's Northeast* (Cosimo 2005), and it is not the purpose of this book to go into detail regarding the history of the stone chambers. It is important at this point that the reader make the connection to the idea that the mysterious stones mark the areas of UFO activity and perhaps Allen Hynek's "windows."

ENCOUNTER WITH THE "RED EYES"
AT A STONE CHAMBER

There were many reported encounters with strange creatures, humanoid beings, UFOs, and ghost lights around the chambers; these are documented in my book *Celtic Mysteries*; however, one recent case that was not published in the book stands out because it is more than a simple UFO encounter. For years, contactees and other UFO researchers who dabble in the occult have warned me about cases that involve the "red eyes," that is, humanoid creatures with glowing red eyes that are dressed in robes and seem to be always up to no good. This incident as well as several others took place in a lonely isolated area in Southeast, New York, called Reservoir Road at about 11:30 p.m. on March 25, 2005. In the past, Reservoir Road and the nearby area has been the scene of many UFO sightings (fig. 14, disk-shaped UFO photographed near Reservoir Road), spook lights, and close encounters with strange beings. There is also a small stone chamber off the north side of the road, which is a favorite hangout for the local Wiccan

Figure 14. Disk-shaped UFO seen in
daylight near Brewster, New York, in 1984.

population, since they claim it is a place of powerful earth
energy. The witnesses were two women, ages thirty-five and
thirty-eight (Beth and Cathy), both registered nurses who decided to take a drive around the reservoir one evening after
work. The following is their story as told to me on April 26,
the same year of their encounter.

CATHY AND BETH'S ENCOUNTER

"On March 24 of this year [2005], we had just finished the
evening shift at the hospital. We are both nurses there and it
was a very stressful night, so after work we decided to take a
ride around the reservoir because it is beautiful this time of
the year since the trees are still bare and you could see the
moon reflecting off the water.

"We first went down to Route 6 to get a quick bite to eat and noticed how clear the sky was. There was a full moon in the sky and it was very bright, next to the moon was this bright star-like object that was changing color from red to blue to green. I pointed the star out to Beth and although it looked strange, we didn't think too much about it. We then got back into the car and headed toward the reservoir. When we came to a clearing, we noticed that the 'star' had moved and shifted its position. It was no longer near the moon—it seemed to be following us. At that time, Beth said that it was only a plane and not to worry. You see, we heard about all the UFO sightings in this area, and I have to admit we were a little spooked when the star started moving in the sky.

"We turned down Reservoir Road and heard a buzzing sound, which got louder and louder. I thought there was something wrong with the car, so I stopped and pulled over to the side of the road. I turned off the engine and we got out of the car, but the noise was still there and it was vibrating our heads. At that moment, Beth said, 'There's that light in the sky.' This was freaky since the light was right over our heads. As we looked at it, the light seemed to be getting lower and lower, and I could tell now it was about six lights in the shape of a triangle. We jumped back into the car, but the car would not start, then all of a sudden, off to the right in the woods, we heard a sound like an army was marching through the brush. We looked and saw the outlines of about ten or more things that had glowing red eyes. Beth screamed and said, 'What the hell is that?' But all we could see were these outlines in the dark, partially illuminated by the moon, with two red eyes on each of them glowing like hot coals.

"I finally got the car started, and when I put it into gear, it bucked and hesitated as if it was going to die. I prayed to God, 'Please don't let the car die.' Beth was screaming that the creatures were all around us. I told Beth to lock the doors—by now at least eight of these creatures were around the car. They were as high as the top of the windows on the car and dressed in hoods and tight black-like jump suits. Their faces were dark and heads were round, but what really scared us were the eyes—they glowed red. They were trying to get in the car, I think to take us. Finally the car stopped hesitating and we sped away. I looked back in the rearview mirror, and the creatures and the UFO were gone, like they just vanished into thin air.

"While the creatures were around the car, we didn't notice the object in the sky, most likely because we didn't look since we were both terrified of what was taking place. We arrived home about midnight, and we both live alone so we spent the night at my place wondering if we should call the police. We finally did, and the desk officer talked to me like I was crazy or drunk and laughed, so we decided not to say anything to anyone else. That night and the nights to follow were terrifying for both of us, because we thought that the creatures would find us and finish what they were trying to do, and that was to take us to their ship."

Since that close encounter, Beth and Cathy did not have any more sightings, but they had "strange" dreams of being taken out of their home by the creatures with the red eyes and being taken into some type of room where they were placed on a table. Both women had similar dreams, and I advised them to seek the help of a psychologist that I work with who treats people who experience trauma from paranormal experiences. This case is still open, and I hope to have more information soon.

THE LOST MINES

Reservoir Road and nearby Upper and Lower Magnetic Mine Roads are very unusual places indeed. The entire area of Southeast and Brewster, New York, are catacombs with underground passages left over from the mining days of the eighteenth and nineteenth centuries (fig. 15, underground passage and mine in Brewster, New York). In the past, residents and police officers have seen "little man-like creatures" on the roads running into the entrance of the mines. There

Figure 15. One of the many underground passages and mines in Brewster, New York.

have also been a number of cases where the hooded beings with the red eyes appear to walk out of the many outcrops of solid iron-rich rocks in that area as if moving in and out some type of doorway. As they are walking through the rock, these beings do not appear solid, but become very solid and physical when they grab hold of their intended subjects (or victims). I know of no incident where someone was taken through what appeared to be an interdimensional doorway, but that does seem to be their intention when they encounter a late-night walker admiring the view of the reservoir.

According to local and state police records, over the past ten years a number of people have mysteriously disappeared in the counties of Putnam and Westchester in New York (source: missing persons reports, New York State Police files, and public records from 1980 through 2000). I wonder if the hooded beings are responsible for a percentage of these disappearances, or perhaps some of these people accidentally slipped through a dimensional "window" when it opened. Since not one of these missing people have returned or been found, I guess we shall never know.

In 1995, I surveyed and explored the mines with my research partner Marianne Horrigan, and although we didn't find any trace of the humanoid creatures, we did find new tunnels, indicating that the mines were used after they were officially closed in 1899. The new tunnels looked quite different than the older ones, since they appeared much smoother, as if made by modern high-tech drills. As of the writing of this book, someone has sealed off the entrance to one of the mines by using a bulldozer, and it is now impossible to enter. My research into property ownership of the mine locations has

shown that the land around the mines and the mines themselves are now owned by the state and federal government.

UFO cases that involve paranormal phenomena or cases
of high strangeness are not new. They were taking place in
the mid-twentieth century, but many were not being reported
since most researchers—including private organizations, government, and military—were looking for evidence of extraterrestrial spaceships rather than interdimensional travelers,
a concept that could not be accepted at that time. However,
today, since the old methods of looking at the phenomenon
have not uncovered anything, we have to look in a new direction with the hope of getting a better understanding of the
UFO experience.

The interdimensional windows located in the Hudson Valley have many things in common with UFO hot areas around
the world. One major similarity is the presence of magnetic
anomalies, both negative and positive. I have discovered a
measurable increase and decrease in the magnetic field of
Earth in and around the area of the stone chambers, and as
we shall see later, it is no coincidence that UFOs are seen in
close proximity to the magnetic anomaly.

A WINDOW OVER THE OCEAN

Portals or windows to another reality most likely exist in a
number of locations on this planet and throughout our known
physical universe. The Bermuda Triangle, which is located
somewhere in the mid-Atlantic Ocean, has long been associated with missing aircraft, ships, people, and UFOs. Although
the area of the Triangle is vast, the actual portal that opens

up may be very tiny, perhaps less than the size of a football field or smaller. People and objects that disappear may enter another reality or a wormhole and become caught between the dimensions, where time is at a standstill. This limbo or barrier between the two dimensions may act as a buffer to protect the two realities from contaminating each other.

The dimensional portal of the Bermuda Triangle might be used by the intelligence behind the UFO phenomenon to enter our world. This is not to say that they are not capable of making artificial wormholes, but that would require a great deal of energy. From reports that I have collected over thirty years, it seems that the UFO intelligence may wait until the portal naturally opens to enter our universe and leave when it opens again. This could explain why UFOs stick around an area for a specific length of time then disappear and then reappear months or years later in a regular cycle. The interdimensional UFO intelligence might also be able to trigger an opening by generating an electromagnetic pulse, forcing a natural portal to open. However, this as stated requires energy and could explain why UFOs are seen around high-tension power lines. In the past, nuts-and-bolts UFO researchers thought that UFOs were "stealing" our electricity to take back to their planet, which is a ridiculous idea. Why would an intelligence that is capable of traveling the universe and adjacent dimensions want a primitive power source like electricity?

During my investigations in the Hudson Valley, I collected a great number of reports of UFOs over locations both human-made and natural that produce an electromagnetic field or pulse. It seems to me that what they seem to be doing is collecting and storing electromagnetic energy in some sort of giant condenser to be used as a blasting pulse to trigger the opening of a dimensional window. The Bermuda Triangle "window" or portal seems to be cyclic, and my research has shown that most of the disappearance takes place during the months of March, July, August, and October. It is also interesting to note that the majority of paranormal and UFO cases also peak at this time.

BERMUDA TRIANGLE CASE STUDIES

The Bermuda Triangle has been known as The Devil's Triangle, The Trapezium of the Damned, The Sea of the Lost or Lost Souls, the Sargasso Sea, and many others. Since the waters are known for calm seas and good weather, scientists are at loss to explain why so many ships, aircraft, and people have vanished in this area. In the eighteenth and nineteenth centuries, the captains of ships avoided this location because of stories of a sea monster that would, without warning, rise out of the calm sea and pull down unsuspecting ships.

The story of the Bermuda Triangle began long ago at the time of Columbus. The explorer mentions in journals that this area of the Atlantic was very calm and quiet; he compared the feeling in that location with the silence of death. On one night, he and his crew saw a greenish glowing light that moved about the sky and under the water. Two years later, after his first trip to the "New World," Spain sent twenty-seven ships on an expedition across the Atlantic to Hispaniola. While passing through the Bermuda Triangle, the skies went from sunny and fair to black and stormy in a few minutes. Of the twenty-seven ships, only seven made it through the Triangle. The captains of the surviving ships tell of a terrifying tale of strange rain that fell straight from the sky and was red to purple in color, of "lightning" without thunder, and winds that seemed to change direction and temperature almost instantly. At times, the rain came down so hard that it ripped the flesh off the men and poked out their eyes. The captains and the crews watched as the twenty ships of their fleet just disappeared one at a time. Then, without warning, the storm was gone and the sky was once again blue and the sea calm.

Modern-day historian Samuel Morison (1887–1976), in his book *Admiral of the Ocean Sea: A Life of Christopher Columbus*, speculates that the sudden severe weather was a freak squall with hail being blown by the wind with great force. Morison also claims the rain and wind was so fierce during this storm that it cut down visibility, and the frightened sailors did not notice the other ships sinking. Seafaring captains are not easily frightened by storms, but the tales the survivors told when they returned to Spain caused many future ships to avoid that particular route to the New World. It must have been a terrifying experience for those sailors who still believed that they had sailed to the end of the world.

MODERN—DAY DISAPPEARANCES

In the Bermuda Triangle, more planes disappear than ships, and in many of the cases the pilots lose navigation and become disoriented about their location. A Navy Constellation transporter aircraft with forty-two people aboard vanished on October 30, 1954. A massive search of seventy-five ships and planes covered the area with a fine-tooth comb, but found nothing. On October 31, 1954, a United States Navy destroyer was in radio contact with its base while passing through the Triangle. Without warning, the base lost communication with the ship, and it was never found. On November 9, 1956, a twin-engine Navy bomber left Hamilton Airfield for Bermuda. A radio message was picked up by the tower shortly after it entered the Triangle area, then nothing was heard from the pilot again—the plane and its crew of nine men seemed to vanish off the face of the earth. On February 2, 1953, an SOS was received from a British transport plane carrying thirty-three passengers and a crew of six en route to Jamaica. The plane vanished, and two weeks of intensive search revealed no clue as to the fate of the plane or the people aboard. As of the twenty-first century, hundreds of ships and planes have simply vanished in the Triangle. One would think that if something natural, like a storm, were the cause of the disappearance, that pieces of a ship or other evidence would be found, but this is not the case.

THE DEVIL SEA

Another location on our mysterious planet that may be another interdimensional window is the Devil Sea off the east coast of Japan. There are just as many lost ships and planes in the Devil Sea as the Bermuda Triangle. In response to these disappearances, in 1970 the Japanese government sent a research vessel with seventy-five scientists and crew out to investigate the Devil Sea. The crew may have found the answer to its mystery because the ship disappeared without a trace!

After the most extensive air-sea rescue search in that country's history, not even a small piece of debris was found.

The Devil Sea and the Bermuda Triangle have more in common than the vanishing ships and planes. Both areas emit strong electromagnetic pulses that cause compasses to spin wildly and jam navigation systems in ships and aircraft. They are also the locations of meteorological phenomena such as swirling clouds, intense electrical storms, and water spouts that appear without warning. These weather anomalies have also been observed in the Hudson Valley as mini tornadoes, dust devils, and ball lightning.

The rotating and swirling air and water is most likely due to a vortex caused when a dimensional window opens or closes. Vortexes are used to describe a similar phenomenon in Sedona, Arizona, where another "window" may be present. This "doorway to the spirit world" was known to exist for centuries by the Hopi Native Americans.

SEDONA: A BRIDGE TO ANOTHER REALITY

I visited Sedona back in the summer of 2001 to research the many claims of paranormal phenomena, and although it is in the United States, there is a feeling as if you have been transported to another reality. Sedona, Arizona, has had its share of UFO sightings. It has become a hot spot in North America where otherworldly encounters are commonplace.

Sedona is located in a valley surrounded by red rock canyons that give it the look of an alien world. The cliff dwellings of the vanished Anasazi Native Americans of Chaco and Four Corners are not very far away, and they were on my list of things to see that summer. Why and how these ancient American tribes vanished is a mystery to this day; however, the Hopi Indians of Sedona claim that UFOs were involved. The Hopi believe that they came to Earth from the sky and claim that soon the people who are still faithful to the tribe will be lifted to a new world just before this one is destroyed.

Many of the Hopi faithful watch the skies every night, waiting for the return of the great sky ship that will take them away to the Promised Land and paradise. Although this belief is very similar to the Christian rapture and Judgment Day, it was the cornerstone of the Hopi religion long before Christianity arrived in North America, and it still is.

A STORY TOLD BY THE ANCIENTS

The story of the ships from the sky was deciphered in ancient rock carvings and pictographs near Mishongnovi, Arizona. The paintings, which have been dated as being over four thousand years old, show a dome-shaped object coming down from the sky, gathering up the faithful. Elders in the Hopi community have said that they believe that the UFOs seen in Sedona have a direct connection with the rock carvings and feel strongly that they are the spirits who are starting to let themselves be known, since they believe that Judgment Day is at hand.

The Hopi also believe that when a person's body dies, his or her spirit goes into another world (dimension) through a vortex located in the Sedona Valley where it lives a new life, or it may come back to this world and reincarnate. The Kachina doll is said to represent certain spirits that come from these other dimensions into our world. During my journey to Arizona, I studied a number of Kachina dolls very carefully, and they are strange indeed! To me they appear to be more than the imagination of an ancient people; they look like what Europeans and people of the Middle East have been calling aliens, demons, jinn, and angels.

People who have visited Sedona report that the area has a certain "feel" to it. While in the locations where the vortexes are said to exist, psychics claim their abilities increase and ordinary people develop temporary psychic powers. There are many New Age groups from the Northeast United States that travel out to Sedona with the hope of having an otherworldly contact. They camp out in a vortex location for days, where they claim to communicate with beings from other dimensions and channel information. What all these interdimensional vortex and window areas have in common around the world is that they all sit right on top of a number of magnetic anomalies with an intermediate electromagnetic pulse. These magnetic anomalies have been recorded by the last Geophysical Year Survey, and maps of their intensity and location can be obtained by contacting the Bureau of Government Publications branch of the National Archives.

REAL STARGATES

In the Hudson Valley, with the help of Dr. Bruce Cornet, I have studied the magnetic anomalies in the areas of high strangeness and in the proximity of a stone chamber or standing stone. We found a great deviation in the magnetic field of Earth as we approached the chamber. In some areas, the compass would also deviate 180 degrees in the opposite direction.

We are not the only ones who discovered this unusual magnetic phenomenon—the government also knows about it. During the last geophysical year, scientists charting changes in the magnetic field of Earth discovered a magnetic anomaly with great intensity just outside the chamber on Reservoir Road in Southeast-Brewster, New York. This anomaly is the largest in the Northeast, and on air aviation maps it is listed so that pilots can avoid it so that it will not affect their navigation instruments. This must mean that the anomaly reaches to great altitudes.

There is no coincidence that the magnetic anomaly is very close to the site of a stone chamber with quite a few cases of UFO sightings and other forms of paranormal phenomena. In the locations of the anomalies, I also discovered an occasional electromagnetic pulse (EMP), which seems to create an invisible vortex felt by animals and human beings. Although the magnetic anomaly is present all the time, the EMP and vortex are periodic. If we can assume that the EMP and the vortex create and generate the paranormal phenomena, then we can get a better understanding why it periodically peaks at certain times of the year.

I have been studying the relation between magnetic anomalies, the vortex, and the appearance of paranormal phenomena for quite a number of years, and the correlation is undeniable. Theoretically, by changing the frequency of the EMP, the vortex can be tuned to open a window to different places in the universe or other dimensions just like in the movie and television series *Stargate*.

RADIO STATION KNOCKED OUT BY EMP

On July 7, 2001, at about 10:00 a.m., radio station WJKM in Hartsville, Tennessee, was knocked off the air by a very powerful blast of unknown energy. The weather was clear—no storms were in the area and there was not a cloud in the sky. All the station's telephone lines were knocked out, several transformers for four blocks had exploded, and all the computers in the station lost their mother cards and main frame. When the employees at the station went outside to try and find some explanation, they found scores of dead birds that seemed to have been burnt. Their wings, tails, and feet were roasted. The editor of a local newspaper next door to the radio station said that she was sitting with her back to the window when she heard a loud roaring sound, and then there was a flash of light that was so bright it went through the entire building.

The power company and BellSouth were at a loss for an explanation as to what caused the power overload. That same evening, numerous residents in Hartsville and the surrounding towns reported strange globes of lights in the sky performing "erratic" maneuvers. Some residents feel that the government was doing some type of experiment in the old Hartsville nuclear plant, since many have seen black helicopters and C-130 transport aircraft land somewhere in the closed facility.

In the days to follow, listeners to the station called in about hearing strange humming sounds and feeling like insects were crawling up and down their skin and the hair standing up on the back of their necks. One person claimed that while holding a fluorescent light bulb in his hand, it lit up. This can only happen when the bulb is exposed to an electromagnetic pulse. In my laboratory at the school where I teach, I perform this experiment by turning on a small tesla coil. This instrument generates a high-frequency, low-energy electromagnetic pulse and wave. If you bring the fluorescent bulb within a certain distance of the coil, the bulb will light as if plugged in to an electric socket. . . .

The Hartsville EMP blast also generated a great deal of other phenomena and physically affected a great number of people who live within three miles of the station. Several people had reported that they had seen a strange "Bigfoot"-like creature roaming the countryside, while others claim to have seen ghosts in their home and on the highways. However, most people reported an increase in irritability and headaches. At night, residents reported that there was a strange smell in the air like ozone. The formation of the ozone molecule (three atoms of oxygen held together in a nonpolar covalent bond) takes place when oxygen is exposed to an electromagnetic or electrical field.

What happened in Hartsville also happened in Montauk Point, Long Island, the Hudson Valley, and Pine Bush, New York. Some paramilitary or secret government agency, or perhaps aliens, seem to be doing experiments with high-frequency generators to create an electromagnetic pulse to perhaps form a vortex and open up a "window." This would also explain the reports of paranormal phenomena and the physical and psychological effects on humans and animals in these locations.

GOVERNMENT EXPERIMENTS

As mentioned before, the intelligence behind the UFOs appear to generate an EMP to create a vortex to open up a dimensional window. It could very well be that a secret project in the military may have also tried this sometime in the late forties with limited success.

Using some of the technology that was thought to be obtained from the Roswell alien ship crash, a secret government project began to unfold somewhere around 1948. This project was called "Project Invisibility," and it involved making objects invisible by warping space around them. High-frequency generators were used, and the device was developed at Princeton University. The first time the device was used, it didn't work, because the system required too much power. When the power problem was solved, there were some unexpected results. It seems that humans were unable to enter the field that was being generated, because they became disoriented. What was taking place was that the electromagnetic radiation was somehow short-circuiting the electrical impulses between the synapses in the brain. In some cases, madness took place and then death. However, when the power of the device was increased, strange lights began to appear in the room and there were even stories of strange images appearing, images of what seemed to be Earth's past.

Had the government created some type of bridge between the present and the past? They were unconcerned with the materializing images since the device produced the desired effect. Objects placed in the test area disappeared, and when the device was turned off, they reappeared in perfect condition. The device worked well with nonliving things, but living creatures seemed to suffer greatly. When the experiment was performed using something living (some type of animal was often used), the living creature would vanish and not return.

It is not known why they decided to go ahead and test it on a Navy ship with a full crew; perhaps someone thought they had solved the problems with living matter. The test was done sometime before 1950, on a ship off the Gulf of Mexico. This experiment was wrongly named the Philadelphia Experiment and was publicized in a number of books and two movies. However, the material that has been made available to the public was mostly misinformation. The ship was not named the Philadelphia, and the location was not off the East Coast as one might expect.

The equipment placed in the ship consisted of a number of high-frequency generators, but the power source that activated these devices is unknown. It is suspected that it was nuclear or something else obtained from the alien technology. The generators were turned on and the ship not only visually vanished, but it also was lost on radar. The ship had a transmitter placed aboard, which sent out a coded signal so that the ship could be tracked; however, when the ship disappeared, so did the signal. Several seconds later, the signal was once again received, but the ship was now almost fifty miles east of its previous location.

Naval Intelligence hurried to locate the ship, which was now near the west coast of Florida, and when they boarded it, they found something very strange. First of all, the electrical equipment on the ship was not working properly or was destroyed. The ship itself looked like it had been through a battle, with considerable structural damage, but the most terrifying thing they were to discover concerned the crew. A considerable percentage of the crew was unaccounted for, including the captain. Many of the crew members were behaving like raving lunatics. Further medical examination showed that their brains seem to have experienced some type of sensory overload. There were several crew members who survived and seemed to be in fairly good shape. When the surviving crew was interrogated by officers of Naval Intelligence, they were asked how all this could take place in the few seconds that they had vanished. The crew looked puzzled, since according to them, they were gone for weeks (or months, they weren't sure). It seems that a strange dilation of time took place, and wherever they went, time was running at a different rate.

One of the most amazing things that they talked about was meeting a strange race of beings. They claimed that they actually went into another universe that was void of sensation or anything else. There were no trees, there was no water, and there was no sun in the sky. They said that they were in some type of glowing yellow-white fog that looked like the Christian version of limbo, a place between heaven and hell. In this limbo, they said that a number of strange creatures approached them and came aboard the ship. These beings looked like giant insects, but they stood upright and were able to communicate with the crew. The crew described how they became like laboratory animals and this is why most of the crew was missing, dead, or insane. The beings wanted to know more about us, so they used the crew of the ship for experiments. The strange beings also seemed interested in our world, but didn't seem to have a way to get here. The experiment allowed us to enter their world; it was like a window that could only be opened from our side. How they finally got back they really didn't know—they just found themselves once again aboard the ship and back in the water.

Although this story sounds unbelievable, it was told to me by Dr. Hynek sometime in 1984. In the late seventies, Dr. Hynek secretly met a person in Mexico who only identified himself as "Carlos." Carlos claimed to be an ex-officer in the Navy with the rank of "commander" and was part of this "Project Invisibility." Although he was skeptical of the story, Dr. Hynek was convinced "Carlos" was telling the truth as he knew it. When Allen Hynek told me this story, I was very surprised, since he always tried to maintain a conservative view of the UFO phenomenon. As Dr. Hynek said, "You can't tell anyone of things like this, especially the media, because they will have a field day with it. We have to keep UFO research respectable, since it's hard enough for mainstream science to accept even a simple UFO sighting."

I also heard other stories from ex-military personnel about interdimensional beings that have been moving in and out of our reality for some time, collecting information for what some feel is an invasion. Many of these reports (or tall tales) center on Pine Bush, New York, where there is a strong military presence. Some residents feel that the government is trying to capture one of these dimensional travelers to obtain their technology.

SIX

THE PSYCHIC CONNECTION

People who have psychic abilities seem to be able to sense the location of a window when the interdimensional vortexes are formed. In my early years of research, I often stayed away from psychics because my scientific training told me that if something can't be measured, you must question its existence. Psychics do claim extraordinary things; however, in college I was told that extraordinary claims require extraordinary evidence, or "if you show me, I will believe it." Over the years I have gained great respect for the psychic community and although I still have my doubts about a number of practicing psychics, there are some who have proved to me that they have the ability to see beyond the physical universe.

People with psychic ability seem to be able to sense when UFOs are around, and they seem able to predict when they will appear in an area. They also are able to predict paranormal phenomena before it takes place, and some claim that they can channel aliens, angels, or people who have passed over. There are most likely millions of people in the United States alone that possess kinetic, potential, or even dormant psychic ability. Since the minds of the people in this country are more open than they were in the fifties and early sixties, many once-dormant psychics have had their abilities awaken and are now able to develop and use their gift without fear of ridicule.

The respect that I have today for psychics is because of a person by the name of Loretta Chaney. Loretta, along with her husband Scott, worked with me on a number of paranormal cases and without their insight and help, I most likely would not have gathered the extent of information about an investigation. Loretta has the ability to communicate with beings from other dimensions and pass on information from those who have crossed over. She also can sense magnetic fields and has had multiple out-of-body experiences. As skeptical as I have tried to be regarding her abilities, she has always surprised me and made me think and evaluate situations a little further than my scientific training allowed me to do. In short, when that part of me, the scientist, said, "Show me to convince me," Loretta always did.

LORETTA'S STORY

Loretta's psychic experiences go back to the time when she was a child. While asleep, she frequently found herself separated from her physical body. She was also able to visit other dimensional realities beyond our own and interact with the people who exist there. Unfortunately, Loretta had difficulty relating to these experiences since they were not accepted at the time in our western culture. Whenever Loretta tried to talk about these experiences to anyone, she would be told that they are "just dreams."

In 1979, she began experiencing bouts of severe dizziness. This condition interfered with her ability to do the simplest things, such as sitting, walking, or driving a car. Weeks of hospital tests proved negative, and Loretta feared that she might not fully recover. A friend suggested that she visit a psychic medium that had helped her with difficulties in the past. At first Loretta was reluctant to go, since what she knew about psychics and psychic phenomena is what she saw in the movies, and it frightened her. However, despite her fears, she was desperate to learn more about her condition, so she decided to go. This decision would change Loretta's life.

During her reading with a spiritualist medium, Loretta was told that the dizziness she was experiencing was not the result of a medical condition, but rather the result of "surgical" work being done on her by doctors from the other side. Loretta was told she was being opened up as a channel of communication between this world other planes of reality and that she would soon begin doing psychic readings. The medium encouraged Loretta to begin classes in psychic development to help accelerate this "opening" and help her to better understand what was happening to her. Loretta decided to take the medium's advice and look for people who were able to teach her more about what was taking place and how it was changing her life.

The morning after her first class, while in bed, Loretta had a fully conscious out-of-body experience, her first since childhood. Contact with the other side had begun again and soon after, these contacts started on a daily basis. Every time Loretta fell asleep she would be out of her body, and during this time she would experience full consciousness. Once again, Loretta was traveling into dimensional realities beyond our own. As her fully conscious out-of-body experiences continued, she was able to accumulate information about the other side and the people and other beings who reside in the different dimensional planes. Meanwhile, the "physicians" on the other side continued to work on her, and several years later she developed the ability to heal and communicate with those who have passed over to the other side.

As stated earlier, I have worked with Loretta in the past many times and although many psychics claim that they can do amazing things, Loretta does not boast about her abilities. She is able to sense different types of energy and changes in magnetic fields, and her ability to heal has been noted in letters from two local doctors. Loretta will not get involved in the channeling of interdimensional entities and so-called extraterrestrials because she knows the dangers involved in such contacts and will try to persuade less experienced psychics to be careful. Loretta told me that she is protected and helped by higher spiritual beings that she calls "guides." The guides help her stay on the path in life she is supposed to travel and assist her in developing her psychic abilities. There is no doubt in my mind that Loretta is in contact with a number of different intelligences from other realities. If you wish to contact her you will find her e-mail and web address in the appendix.

PSYCHICS AND UFOS

Many psychics have reported an encounter with a UFO and/or had a contact experience with one or more types of beings in the middle of the night. Many of the experiences reported to me are the same: they are awakened between two and four in the morning by a light that is often described as green or a very pale white. In most cases the light has no source, and it is usually emitted from the head of the being(s). There are many descriptions of the types of entities that have been seen: tall grays, short grays, tall Nordic-looking beings that appear almost human, and finally creatures that resemble a reptile or giant insect. In most cases, when people open their eyes, they are paralyzed and the only part of their body that they can move is their eyes or head. A letter was sent to me a number of months ago from an individual known as "Charles." Charles has been aware of his psychic abilities since he was very young, and as a child he thought it was a common thing with all people.

CHARLES'S PSYCHIC ENCOUNTER

Charles is a thirty-five-year-old male who had some incredible experiences in his youth. As a young child of six years, he had recurring dreams of being abducted by some type of craft in the sky. The dream always began the same: He is outside playing and the sky is dark, but there is an orange glow. He knows that he is not supposed to be outside, and his parents would get angry and punish him if they knew. How he got outside he doesn't know, but the "dream" starts the same way each time with him outside playing. Then a bright yellow light appears in the sky and it seems to be coming closer and closer. He starts to run and looks back and sees the light getting lower and brighter. He can make out its shape now, and it's like a box in the sky with lights around the center. He looks up and sees "a man" looking down from one of the windows. The man tells him, "Do not run. We have come for you." He then falls, and the next thing he knows, he wakes up in bed and it is morning.

This "dream" repeated itself at least twice a month until his eighth birthday and then it stopped. One morning after the dream, his mother yelled at him for dirty hands and nails. She asked him how he got his hands dirty, and he told her, "Trying to hold on to the ground so that the star man can't take me." On a number of nights, while still a child, he would walk in his sleep, and one time his parents woke up in the middle of the night from the sound of a door being slammed and found Charles walking in from outside.

When Charles was ten years old, he claimed he could "feel" what people were thinking and often heard voices telling him things about science and about other worlds. Several months after his twelfth birthday, Charles woke up in the middle of night to find his room illuminated by a pale green-white light. At the foot of the bed were two beings who were just staring at him. The beings were very tall and had long blonde hair, and their eyes glowed with a blue light. They were wearing robes that were green, blue, and white, and their fingers seemed much longer than those of a man or a woman. He then tried to move but was paralyzed. After what seemed like a long time, one of the beings "floated" over to him and put his hand on Charles's head. When the being did this, he felt a vibration in his entire body and he seemed to pass out.

The night visitations continued until he was fourteen. When he tried to tell someone about them, including his parents, he was told they were just dreams. On one occasion, he went to see a priest at the local church and told him the story of the beings in his room. The priest told him not to be afraid because they were angels and they are protecting him because he must have a great purpose in life. That made Charles feel better, and he was no longer afraid of the "angels" who came to him at night. From that moment on, he kept the future visitations by the beings and the sightings of strange lights in the sky to himself.

Charles now lives in California. He continues to have encounters with UFOs and channels information from the "angels" to various groups. One of the extra- or ultraterrestrials that he channels is called Monka, who has popped up more than once during my research.

MONKA AND THE PYRAMIDS OF MARS

Monka was first channeled in the 1960s by a group of psychics that called themselves the Solar Cross Foundation. Since that time, at least a dozen or more channelers have claimed communication with Monka. During my research, I have personally interviewed and talked to Monka through three different psychic mediums. It could very well be that all three of them had heard the tapes put out by the Solar Cross Foundation and just consciously or subconsciously continued to spread the messages of Monka. The messages from Monka are all very similar despite the fact that the first tape was made over forty years ago and one would think that he would have something new to say in that length of time. However, there was one channeling session that I attended where a psychic phenomenon was generated as a result of the communication with Monka, and to this day I am still convinced that some intelligence other than the psychics' own imagination was communicating with those who attended the session that evening.

I was invited to a group channeling session on August 21, 2002, in New York City. Normally I would not go to such a gathering, since 90 percent of the time they turn out to be a waste of time. What made me travel from Connecticut to the Big Apple was the fact that the psychic channel was claiming to be in contact with Monka and a number of other ET entities. Well, it'd been a while since I'd heard from Monka, so I had to attend the group to find out what was going on. Those of you who are interested in my first encounter with Monka can find it in my book *Contact of the 5th Kind* (Llewellyn 1997).

I arrived early and knew a number of the people there, so we had a relaxing drink (nonalcoholic) and discussed what the group was going to attempt that evening. Most of the people that were present, twenty-five or so in all, were practicing psychics. The person who was going to channel was named Brett (I never found out his last name), and the group flew him in from Florida to give an evening "performance" to this gathering.

I have a reputation of being open-minded, but very analytical in my research; however, as I said earlier, extraordinary claims require extraordinary evidence. This evidence or burden of proof has to come from the person channeling, and he must prove that the being talking through him is not of this Earth. Unlike many of the people who attend this type of gathering, to me it's not a matter of faith, but a matter of proof. This evidence can be in the form of scientific information, but such would not be the case this evening. The evidence would appear in the form of a number of physical manifestations.

At 7:30 p.m., we all settled down on the floor and Brett came out and started to talk with us. I had never met him or heard of him before, so I thought to myself, *Hey, this might turn out to be something since this guy is not seeking any publicity.* It has been my experience that those psychics and channelers that seek out the media and try to make a name for themselves are usually fakes trying to make a quick buck (some channelers charge people one hundred dollars or more to attend their sessions) or people frustrated with their own lives and looking for an audience to make themselves feel important. After about ten minutes of silence, Brett's facial features started to change, and it appeared as if he had difficulty breathing. I did get a little concerned at that time; however, a moment later he relaxed and just sat there with his eyes closed as if meditating.

Then, without warning, the temperature of the room dropped, and not by a few degrees—it was a hot August day and it got cold in that room. One of the people sitting next to me said, "My God, what's going on? This never happened before." The room got so cold that I could see my breath. I had experienced this effect before during my first encounter with Monka, as the entity channeled through a couple in Greenwich, Connecticut—there also the room got very cold. I believe that the drop in room temperature was caused by the entity drawing energy, not only from the molecules in the air, but also from the heat energy radiating from the bodies of those present.

Then Brett began to speak. He said that Monka was there, but had not taken over his body yet. He wanted us to know that he was aware of a new presence (I guess that was me), someone whom he had communicated with before and who is in contact with a higher being. I wonder if he was referring to my first contact with Monka, where a higher angelic being called "Donestra" used Monka to get a message to me. Donestra is an alleged angelic entity who channeled the most amazing technical diagrams through a Mr. Dean Fagerstrom (fig. 16, one of thirty-two diagrams channeled by Dean Fagerstrom). This story and my "contact" with Dean and Donestra are also covered in detail in *Contact of the 5th Kind*. The story of Dean and Donestra is too lengthy to mention here.

After fifteen or so minutes, the room was still chilly, I would say no warmer than forty degrees. When Brett started channeling Monka, there was a notable change in his voice and the accent was I would say Indian or Middle Eastern. It seems that most channelers use this type of accent, and I guess if you are channeling a great wise master, this type of voice is more convincing than a Brooklyn or Southern accent. Monka then told the group that he was part of a fed-

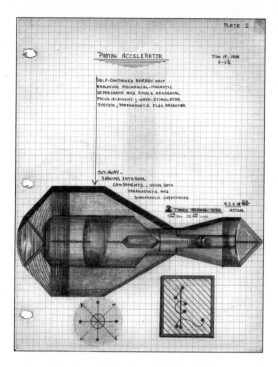

Figure 16. Alien device channeled from "Donestra"
through Dean Fagerstrom in 1968.

eration of planets and that they have been interested in our
world and the living beings that exist here for many hundreds of centuries. He said that there were others present
with us that night, and they were all from other planets.
Their names were Kalia, Zar, Soltec, Lomu, Wan, and Or-
vada. Although the channeling session was two hours long
(a record in my book), I will give the highlights of what was
said from the "mind of Monka" the "ET" using the mouth of
Brett the human.

MONKA'S MESSAGE

"Greetings, in the light of our radiant one. My name is Kaddar Monka. I am a guardian of the Earth, and this message is being sent to you from my station under the pyramids of the planet that you call Mars. It is our purpose to illuminate the minds of the human race and help them prepare for a new age that will be coming in your lifetime. The entire universe, both the physical and nonphysical, is bound together by energy, and when we are out of love and understanding, we are out of harmony with our creator.

"My space brothers and I would like to discuss with you a number of things tonight. As many of you know, we possess more than one body. We are three in number: the astral, physical, and spiritual. In our waking hours, we use the physical body and in sleep we project our astral body outward. What you call a dream is in reality your astral body experiencing its existence in the other realms of the higher planes. The astral body can travel to any part of the universe instantaneously. When you have dreams of flying, you are really astral-traveling through different realms of the universe, both physical and spiritual. During astral travel, you might visit loved ones who have passed over, or you might even visit your space brothers, those highly developed souls that many of you have called guides or angels. Sometimes we come to you during your astral traveling and invite you aboard our ships; here we teach you the things you will need to know for your life and to help your race. We do this also so that when you of the Earth finally meet us in person in the physical form, you will not be frightened of us.

"We are in contact with many others on your planet, teaching them about interstellar communication and inspiring them to develop new technologies that will help you grow. Many of you on this planet have had encounters with UFOs. Most of them are part of our federation; however, a small few are not and contact with them should be avoided, since they are out for their own purpose and have no intention of helping humanity.

"From the time of birth, many of you in this room and across your planet have consented to work with us. We visited you as a child and placed the spark in you to search for the truth, to look beyond what your physical senses tell you. Your space brothers can also travel in their astral bodies, although many times when they meet with an Earth person they are in their physical form. Many of you that have had astral visits with us have been healed of illness and injury to your soul, spirit, and physical body. Negative thinking results in creating a negative environment. All of our bodies are influenced by the others; the physical body is the most difficult to train since it is filled with many desires that can hinder your growth.

"We are a spiritually and technologically advanced society, a federation of planets across the known universe. We who have signed in at this time include Lira, Binta, Ursulus, and Hatton, who are also assigned to the Earth and are its keepers. The astral body leaves and enters the physical body through the top of the head at the crown chakra. It can travel through and around physical objects and most humans in the physical state cannot see it, although many can sense its presence. The role of the astral body in the development of your race is two-fold. The first is to help the physical body to discover its life work, and the second is to protect the physical body from illness and danger from certain other life forms that exist close to you, but in a different dimension.

"During pre-birth, the astral body is busy preparing for the entry into the physical body. At death, the astral body then returns and passes the physical life it lived to see if it achieved the goals asked of it. If not, it may want to return or reincarnate later back into the physical body to complete its work. Our creator made it so that all three bodies cannot be balanced unless they are in harmony with each other and other beings in the universe.

"Each day, you should set aside a time for meditation and prayer—this is nourishment for the astral and spiritual body and something they cannot exist without. When one enters the sleep stage, it is essential to protect yourself from outside influences. The things you call nightmares may take place because you do not have sufficient protection. Before entering the sleep stage, say a prayer to our creator and ask for the energy of his love to protect you. Most of the fear you have is created by your own mind. Fear as an entity or force does not exist; it is only real to you. If you have hate or anger, then eventually it will manifest as fear. In the sleep stage, fear may appear like horrible monsters trying to destroy you. In order to be in harmony, you must learn to control your fears and see them for what they really are. They are not real."

The communication ended and we were allowed to ask questions. I asked a number of scientific questions, which were not answered correctly (from my point of view). The answers that Monka and the other "space brothers" gave were philosophical in nature and really didn't make too much sense, and they sounded like the long-winded statements of a politician, lawyer, or used-car salesman. The answers I received to my questions really did not satisfy me, but many in the room were nodding their heads up and down as if they understood.

The room was still a bit chilly and when I asked another question Monka seemed to get angry, and at that moment a shelf came crashing down and objects on it went flying across the room. That took me by surprise, but when the lights went out I finally got the word from Monka that I was rocking the boat. As the communication ended and Brett once again became Brett, the lights went on and the room once again returned to its summertime temperature of eighty degrees. I have been at a number of channeling sessions where physical manifestations took place, but this is the first time it seemed to be directed at me in anger. So much for the loving space brothers who live in harmony.

I had a number of problems with the communications from Monka that night; the first is that he often used the term "the Earth." Only a native of this planet would say "the Earth"; after all, when we talk about Mars or Venus we don't call them "the Mars" or "the Venus." A true ET, when referring to our planet, would call it "Earth," not "the Earth." Also Monka mentioned "space brothers" when referring to the beings that run this federation of planets. Are there no space sisters? However, Brett looked like he was somewhere around sixty, and this is a comment I would expect from someone who had grown up in the fifties in a male-dominant society. I cannot explain the paranormal events (the change in temperature and the poltergeist) that took place that night or whether Monka and the federation of space brothers actually exist. I guess for those present that evening, believing is determined by the mind of the beholder.

Psychics have to realize that channeling is like a party line—you have no idea who you are talking to and what their real agendas are. The communications that take place in channeling sessions appear as if someone is playing a cosmic game with the human race. There are legends in many cultures of beings who try to contact the physical world from another plane of reality with the hope of using the energy generated by certain people to create a portal or window into this world. The Native Americans have known these entities as the tricksters, Middle Eastern cultures have called them the jinn, and Western civilization refers to them as demons. It is very possible that some unknown intelligence was using the trusted name of Monka to gain access into our world that night by harvesting the energy of the people attending the session.

THE EXPERIENCES OF
REVEREND MICHAEL CARTER

During the spring of 2005, Joan Carra, a well-known psychic, gave me the name of a person who also had psychic abilities and claimed contact with a number of different types of entities that have appeared to him since he was a child. Reverend Michael Carter is an extraordinary individual whose contact experiences proved to be positive for him and spiritually uplifting. Although he has never seen a UFO in the sky or had a close encounter with an object, he has had multiple contacts with beings that appear in his bedroom that could be inter-dimensional in origin. Reverend Carter gave me permission to use his story, which I am very grateful for because it does shed a great deal of light on the contact phenomenon.

"I was born on planet Earth at 4:09 a.m. in the city of Baltimore, Maryland, on July 9, 1957. My parents were hard-working folk who wanted my brother and me to have an easier time of it than they had when they were growing up during the Great Depression. They did not want us to suffer the slings and arrows of outrageous fortune that life could bring. In this way, they were like most parents who wanted the best for their children. I attended church regularly with no real prodding from my parents. My parents seemed to be delighted that I took such an interest in the church without any pressure from them. This interest and enthusiasm that I had for religion would serve as a backdrop for my contact experiences, as I am one of those people who are not so much interested in the 'nuts and bolts' of the phenomenon. I am not interested in propulsion systems and the like. I do not really have an interest in what makes the ET spacecraft maneuver through time and space (which I assume they do). I am more interested in how the contact experience influences the inner life of the human being that they contact. That is to say, what are the spiritual influences or transformations that occur in the experience after he or she has had the visit?

"Growing up, I did enjoy the church services I attended and took the teachings very seriously. With hindsight now, I am sure that I also wanted to please my parents (as any child would), and so that was also a motivation for my attending services on Sunday mornings. The teachings from the New Testament did give me a sense of inner peace as well as providing me with a model as to how to live my life. I immersed myself into the life of the congregation by singing in the choir, serving as a deacon, and even serving as an acolyte in the Lutheran Church on occasion, as well as attending confirmation classes.

"I recall many times during my early childhood when I would awaken in the morning with blood on my pillow. Not knowing where it came from, I thought perhaps my ears were bleeding during the night. Only later did I realize that my nose was bleeding. I thought nothing of it, except that it was rather strange. I can also recall seeing little orbs of light in my room at all hours of the day and night. They were different colors and, to my child's mind, looked like donuts floating in the air. No one else seemed to notice them but me, and sometimes there were marks, bruises, and scratches on me when I woke up in the morning, but I never really thought about how they came to be there. I rationalized that perhaps I had bumped into something and did not remember doing so. In addition to these anomalies, ever since I can remember, I have always had the ability to perceive various colors around people's bodies and around inanimate objects. Later on in life, I realized that I perceived the human aura or energy field, but as a child and youth I did not have the knowledge or the vocabulary to express these ideas.

"When my contact experiences consciously began on December 28, 1989, I resisted any form of organized religion as I attempted to process my experiences and what they meant to me regarding both religion and my personal spirituality. I became heavily involved in the study of metaphysics and new thought philosophies as a result of my contacts with ET beings. Eventually my religious and spiritual questioning and exploration called to me deeply, especially after my contact experiences. I attended an interfaith seminary to continue my studies on comparative religions and further my reflections about living a spirit-filled life. After graduation, I was ordained an interfaith minister. Later, I would attend Union Theological Seminary and receive a Master of Divinity degree. For a few years I was on the path to being fellowshipped as a Unitarian minister but eventually decided against that affiliation.

"On December 28, 1989, I had a visitation from an extraterrestrial being. Prior to this visitation, I had no interest in science fiction movies or science fiction novels. As a matter of fact, I distinctly recall a conversation I had with a friend while walking along the streets of downtown Baltimore. I do not recall how the subject came up, but he asked me if I believed there was life on other planets. I told him that I did not believe in life on other planets, because it was not mentioned in the Bible. My answer seems so ignorant in hindsight twenty years or so later. Can you imagine? That was my reply at the time because that's what I was taught consciously or unconsciously by society.

"My lady friend at the time (who would later become my first wife) and I had just returned from a vacation in Cancún, Mexico, where we went for a little rest and relaxation and to spend some time on the beach. While vacationing in Cancún, we had taken a day trip to see the step pyramids at Tulum and Chichén Itzá on the Yucatán Peninsula. The trip was fascinating because we learned about the Mayan civilization and their fascination with time as well as astronomy. (To this day the Mayan calendar is the most accurate calendar known to humankind.) We returned home to New York on the evening of the twenty-seventh of December. The next day was pretty uneventful as we were just glad to be home. During the early part of the evening of the twenty-eighth, I got together with some friends to socialize and to discuss our vacation. I left them around 10:00 p.m. to catch the subway home.

"I was fatigued and not yet used to the cold weather in New York after the warmth of ten days in Mexico. My girlfriend and I went to bed around 11:30 p.m. or so; I was so glad to get home and to get into my warm bed. Later, I remember just having to open my eyes and get up for some reason; I do not recall whether it was to go to the bathroom or not. I do recall distinctly not feeling like getting up, as I was warm and comfortable under the blankets, and I am one of those people that sometimes if I wake up during the night and open my eyes, it is very difficult for me to get back to sleep. But there was this persistent feeling that I must open my eyes and get up. Suddenly, despite my resistance, I was wide awake. What I saw really, really, really frightened me! My room was lit up with a bluish white light—lit up like it was daytime. Standing at the end of the bed staring at me was a being with an egg-shaped head and wraparound eyes! (I have heard someone who also saw a similar being describe them as 'Ray-Ban' eyes, like the sunglasses that were popular during the eighties.) This being was just staring at me, and it really freaked me out. I do not believe I have ever been that frightened in all of my life.

"He (it could have been female, but I 'felt' it was a male being) was dressed in a silver tight-fitting jumpsuit or uniform with a tunic collar, just staring at me. At that moment I did what any self-respecting male would do—I pulled the cover over my head and hoped it would go away! As I did this, I heard a whooooshing sound in my ears, almost as if I were in a windstorm. The temperature changed as if I had left the room and was outside for a moment. I forced myself to pull down the covers from my head to see where I was (or rather where he was), and I was lying in bed but the being was not there. It was again dark in my room, and all was eerily quiet. My partner had not even stirred! I attempted to wake her and she would not wake up. I saw that she was still breathing, but it was really bizarre to me that she would not awaken. Yet I do remember going back to sleep afterwards. Later that morning when she awoke, I told her about my experience of the previous night, and fortunately she took it all in stride. Looking back now, that really does not surprise me as she was and is an extremely open and spiritual woman. She never doubted me even when we were later married, which was to prove to be a tremendous support during the years ahead.

"As for me, I was a nervous wreck. From that night on, I would not sleep with the lights out, as I was afraid of what would happen if they came again. Here I was, a grown man, but I would wait until I was just on the verge of sleep and then I would get up and turn off the lights. If my girlfriend was home, I felt a bit more at ease because I was not alone, yet when they returned she could not help me. She was fast asleep. I needed to know just what had, in fact, happened. I needed to be able to talk to someone. I found myself wondering if perhaps there were others who had the same experiences and could resonate with my story. I confided my contact experience to a friend of mine who always seemed to be a guide in my life and who would listen and not judge; she had the uncanny ability to come up with advice that always proved to be sound in the long run. When I told her of my experience, she advised that I travel to the neighborhood known as 'Alphabet City' in the East Village in New York. The neighborhood is called Alphabet City because the streets are named after consecutive letters in the alphabet.

"She told me that when I got to a certain street to look at a particular mural that had been painted and to see if the pictures reminded me of anything. This proved important, as I still was not quite sure of what I saw. There was a part of me that did not want this to be some type of ET being from elsewhere. I wanted a more rational explanation. I took her advice one afternoon and visited this particular neighborhood and, sure enough, someone had painted a mural with pictures of gray aliens! Those images looked exactly like the being I had seen in my bedroom that evening in December. I was relieved, but now I also feared for my sanity. I did not know what to do.

"However, the visits continued for about six months or so, always on the full and new moon. Each visit was frightening to me, even though the beings never harmed me. It was my fear that was the blockage to really experiencing the visits and being able to deal with, instead of react to, my visitors.

Fear keeps us from being in relationship with the world and with ourselves. As I said before, there was no harm done to me. If anything, my worldview started to change, and I was beginning to see a connection with all of life and creation. My views about what people call 'God' and religion definitely shifted to a more inclusive and less anthropomorphic view of who and what the Creator is.

"The visits usually consisted of me lying in bed, attempting to sleep. The room would become eerily quiet, and it seemed that even street noises would cease. The very air became still. At times, it seemed that I would faintly hear a low humming sound in my ears seconds before their arrival. Suddenly and without warning, I would be paralyzed; I could not move or even open my eyes. Instead, they would show me pictures in my head of them being in the room. The pictures were like small computer icons being shown in my head. One being would hold out his hand and a ray would come out and touch me, and I would feel like electricity was going through my whole body. On one visit, I did happen to be lying on my back, and I was wearing a rose quartz, as this stone has a calming effect on me. When the being sent the ray out into me, the rose quartz I was wearing actually cracked, without hurting me at all. Later, I saw that the stone was cracked, but not broken. Unfortunately, I later misplaced the crystal. I do not believe this stone was cracked purposely to damage my property, but the crystal just happened to be in the way when the ray was shot towards me. I was paralyzed and could not readily open my eyes during these visits, but I found that if I focused my concentration, I could force them open. When I did successfully open my eyes, the room would be empty.

"I felt that I clearly needed to speak to someone professional and soon the opportunity presented itself. Albert Einstein was once quoted as saying, 'God does not play dice.' That is to say that there are really no coincidences in the cosmos. As I mentioned, I am a voracious reader and always have been. When these experiences began, I read everything I could on the subject. The very first book I read on the subject was entitled *Encounters* by Edith Fiore, PhD. However, the synchronicity of how I found this book was so profound that even Ray Charles could see this was no coincidence. One late afternoon, I was browsing in a bookstore called the Open Center, located in the SoHo neighborhood of lower Manhattan. As I was glancing at the shelves, I noticed several books on the subject of UFOs. I looked around to see if anyone was paying attention to me and the fact that I was looking at books in this section, because I was feeling extremely embarrassed. I feared (that word again) that someone might think that I was crazy. After I assured myself that I was 'safe,' I picked up several books and Dr. Fiore's was one of them. While glancing through the book, I noticed that in the back, she had a list 'symptoms,' if you will, of what to look for if an individual suspects he or she is having an encounter with an extraterrestrial intelligence. The book also had a list of professional therapists who specialized in clients who were contactees! I felt that I had hit the jackpot, but there was more to come.

"Sheepishly I walked over to the cashier to pay for the books. I felt like a teenager buying condoms for the first time. I could not even look the cashier in the face; I just wanted to pay for the books and get out of there before anyone noticed what I was buying. As he added up the total, he asked me without cracking a smile, 'Is this for real or is this just a hobby?' When I glanced up, he was looking at the book I was purchasing, and he held the *Encounters* book in his hand. I started to lie; I wanted to say, 'Of course not, man. This is something I am just dabbling in. You know I read this crazy stuff from time to time, but the book is not even for me. It is a gift for a really weird friend of mine. You know how it is.' Instead, I answered, 'It is for real.' What he said next was an answer to my unspoken prayers: 'I know a place you can go and be with others like you. It is a support group. If you are interested, I can give you a number to call. I used to go myself.' He gave me the number and I called.

"When I called, they asked me a series of questions before giving me any information. The questions were a kind of screening, I guess, to make sure people coming to the group were not too much on the fringes. Imagine that—other folks more on the fringe than people who say they had contact with ETs. I thought, *go figure* and took the information they provided. Because the *Encounters* book also had a list of therapists who specialized, if you will, in dealing with people who had contact with UFOs and their occupants, I closed my eyes and picked a therapist who used hypnotic regression as a modality to disclose what had happened to me. During our time together, she affirmed my experience and assisted me in coming to grips with what had happened to me.

"The support group—SPACE (Search Project for Aspects of Close Encounters)—turned out to be a godsend. The group was formed in March 1992 by Mr. Harold Egeln. Mr. Egeln had experiences himself, and is very well versed in the phenomena of UFOs and extraterrestrials. I was welcomed with open arms, and the people I met were open about their experiences. Some had even gone public with their encounters. I was definitely not ready for that at the time, and I admired their courage. In the group, there were not only others who had the same and/or similar experiences as myself, there were also other people of color (though not very many) who had experiences as well. Over time, I noticed that although there was varied interest among the individuals in the group concerning the phenomenon itself, most people viewed their encounters as spiritually transformative and positive in their lives. Certainly, there were those in the group who were more interested in the so-called nuts and bolts of the phenomena; that is to say, they were fascinated by the propulsion systems of the craft and so forth. Others were more interested in what the government knew or did not know—what could be labeled 'conspiracy theories.' (I must admit I gravitate towards this subject as well.) Yet overall, the energy of the group was one in which most people had welcomed the experience in their lives despite the ridicule they sometimes endured. Most of the group said the 'visitors' had transformed them spiritually and now claimed their identities as 'cosmic citizens,' if you will. Barriers such as nationality, religion, ethnicity, race, etc., played second fiddle to the identity of being one with all of Creation. This was important to me because I later became aware that different support groups had different personalities or identities.

"The group was just what I needed at the time because the visits continued. I noticed that during the first two or three years of these visits (they continue to this day), they would tend to come more frequently and in clusters during summertime. It was during the summer of 1990 that I had my only visit from a reptilian being. On this particular summer evening, I was lying in bed awake on my back, staring at the ceiling. My partner was again out because she had to work a club date. My ritual of turning out the lights just before I was about to drift off continued, and when I returned to the bed after turning off the light, I rested on my stomach. Suddenly, I felt a weight on my back as if someone or something was sitting on it. I could hardly breathe! I was paralyzed and could not open my eyes. I was terrified and I tried to calm myself by telling myself that it was just them visiting again. (Even today, I still have an initial feeling of fear when I get a visit.)

"While paralyzed with this weight on my back, I was mentally shown a picture of a being that I can only describe as Spider-Man-looking, except that this being was green and had scales with yellowish cat-like eyes. I heard a voice whisper in my ear, saying, 'You're going to be rich and famous' (this has yet to happen, by the way). I forced myself up by sheer will and forced open my eyes. To my astonishment, I watched this being simply walk through my window and outside of the building. I lived on the fifteenth floor at the time! A few nights later, I had a dream in which a being that looked like a giant alligator and walked on two feet was speaking to me, though I never made out what it was saying. These new visitors heightened my fear because I had just barely become accustomed to visits by the so-called grays.

"Before going further, there is something I must say, something else about my experiences. Perhaps it is because I am a person of color in the dominant Eurocentric culture of these United States, but the mere sight of these beings is both awe-inspiring and frightening. They are clearly not from these parts. Yet, I am sensitive to the fact, and I try to remain objective in the realization, that just because a being does not look like me, that does not mean it intends to harm me. I am also aware that objectivity is merely subjectivity under restraint. I mention this because I cannot tell you how many books and articles I have read that indict the so-called grays or reptilians as sinister or evil, while embracing the blonde, blue-eyed Swedes or Pleiadeans as benevolent and loving. These portrayals may or may not be true. Intergalactic racism is a very real phenomenon in my humble opinion and needs to be called out when it is evident. After all, we humans can be pretty xenophobic when it comes to the so-called other.

"A few weeks after my first known contact in December of 1989, this is what happened to me. I was having problems breathing fairly consistently at that time, and a friend of mine suggested that I see a healer. The healer practiced something called 'Reiki.' I started feeling stronger after the first session, and after going once a week for six weeks, I really felt better. The practitioner encouraged me to learn this healing technique, but I refused. Yet within about ten days, I began studying Reiki. That contact changed my life and awakened my realization that I am a healer and that this is what I came here to Mother Earth to do. Now, I use it with my patients at the hospital where I serve as a chaplain, working primarily with cancer patients."

It is interesting to note that Reverend Carter's psychic and healing abilities increased considerably after his encounters with the beings. This would be the case with many individuals whom I talked with over the years. After their initial contact experience, many of them would follow a spiritual path as a healer, teacher, or psychic medium. The next case presented involves one of extraordinary contact. Although it is quite different than Reverend Carter's experiences, it is important since it indicates the complex multidimensional makeup of the contact phenomenon.

INTERDIMENSIONAL CONTACT
SINCE CHILDHOOD

Posey Lee Gilbert is a person whose contact experiences started at the early age of five, and these visitations still continue to this day. Posey has had a number of paranormal experiences and UFO sightings; in fact, he was one of the witnesses of the Hudson Valley UFO. Posey also claims to have communicated with a number of different beings telepathically in the daylight and carried out face-to-face conversations with an ET or dimensional entity. Although he is not a practicing psychic, he without a doubt has the ability to see beyond our physical plane of existence. Posey's story is very long and complex, and of the seventy-five pages sent to me detailing his experiences, I can only focus on those that are relevant to this book.

THE DARK FIGURES

One day, while still a child, Posey walked by his sister's bedroom. She was at school at that time, and he saw three jet-black silhouettes sitting on her bed, two at the head and one at the foot. He stood there, wide eyed and open mouthed, when they suddenly jumped to their feet and began to race around the room at a fantastic speed. They were moving so fast that they looked like vapors swirling around in the air. As they did this, he could hear a sound like flapping. The figures converged on the window, which turned into a black rectangle (a portal opening); they went through and were gone. Before the rectangular window closed, it seemed to be sucking air into it because he heard a whooshing sound. Posey feared that he might also be sucked into it, but then it was gone and the room was back to normal. He then told his mother what he had seen, and she told him not to tell his father when he got home because his father might think he was "crazy."

THE LADY

After the incident with the swirling beings in his sister's bedroom, his mother told him to go to his room and take a nap. While he was lying on the bed, he saw a creature outside the window that he and his brother saw once before, which they called the walking stick because it looked like a giant praying mantis. It was on the rooftop across from their building. He could see the creature standing there in the bright light of the noon sun. He then became aware of a presence in the room and saw a black hand with four fingers slowly rise from under the bed. The fingers were long and pointed and were the same blackness as the silhouette beings that he saw earlier in his sister's room. The four fingers were arranged on the hand with the longest one in the center. (I found this to be an interesting comment since years earlier, someone had sent me a picture of an alleged alien hand that was recovered from the Roswell-Corona crash. The "hand" in the picture looked exactly like what Posey describes seeing as a child).

Posey then became very scared and the next thing he knew, he was out on the roof outside the window. On the roof there was some type of object shaped like a pie plate with a slice-like opening. Standing in front of this opening was a tall man who was very white with light blue, almost gray eyes. His hair was platinum blonde, and he was very muscular and looked graceful. He was over six feet tall, and he had on a skintight suit that looked like spandex. He had on a helmet that looked like those worn by the soldiers of ancient Egypt, but it was not made of metal. There was also a woman and, behind her, another man. They all looked like they were of the same race. He remembered that they all looked very beautiful. "Had it not been for the silver craft that was sitting on the roof," he said, "I would have thought that they were angels."

The woman had no helmet on, and she was very beautiful and had the same muscular build as the men, but different, more feminine. The woman's hair was reddish in color, and her hair was long and hung below her waist. Her eyes were emerald green. (I thought this was also an interesting comment since the Celtic people of long ago described the goddess of Earth as possessing long red hair and green eyes.)

Posey wanted to touch her hair to see if it was as soft as it looked, but he never did. She was the only one who spoke to him, but he doesn't remember what she said, since he was only six years old at the time. He knew they were some type of space people, but he was surprised that they didn't look like what he had seen in the movies at that time—that is, men and women in large, thick suits with glass bubbles on their heads with antenna.

Then "the lady" showed him a number on a circular object and said, "This is the Universal Number. When you align the grooves, you can see into other dimensions of the universe." The next thing young Posey knew, he was in his bed and it was dark. His mother was calling for him to get up and wash his hands for dinner. When he mentioned the encounter with the lady on the roof, his mother told him that it was probably a dream and to stop the nonsense. That was the first time he saw the lady, but not the last time he was to hear from her. As he grew up, he would hear her voice many times, talking to him and guiding his path in life.

THE LONG DREAM

One of the most interesting experiences that Posey had is what he calls the "long dream," since he actually felt the passage of time and the "dream" continued into the next night. It is very possible that he was taken to another dimension, because the incident took place in a crowded area close to New York City and involved a great number of people. It is also very possible that the beings that are dimensional can actually abduct you, taking only your astral body and not your physical body. This may have been the case in Posey's experience. It is presented here with his permission in his own words.

"One night when I was seven years old, I found myself in an empty bedroom, and when I went to my parent's room, I also found them gone. I looked out the window to the street and saw that the street was full of people and they were in lines. I got dressed and went to see if I could find my parents and family in the crowd. When I reached the corner, I saw a policeman and I asked him what was happening. He just kept on staring ahead and pushed me and said, 'Move on.' I saw all the people I knew in the neighborhood, and those with authority were standing on the side and in a droning mantra were saying, 'Move on . . . move on.' There was no traffic, no planes in the sky, but I could see a huge, yellow, mushroom-shaped craft sitting in the baseball field of the park just ahead. I could see that's where everyone was going to. I was the only one who it seemed paid it any mind. Everyone else just walked slowly, with their eyes looking ahead. When I got to the gate of the park, I then saw what my brother Ralph and I called a Saurian. Today, some say it was a reptilian alien, but that's the term we used to describe this type of being.

"When I got to the gate, the Saurian stopped the line and I said, 'You better not be here tomorrow because our Air Force will blow the hell out of you.' It just looked at me and said, 'We will shift into another dimension where you can't see us, but we can see you.' At that point, the 'dream' ended and the next night I had it again, but it began at the point were I was stopped in the line by the Saurian. This time the Saurian pushed me forward and said, 'Move on.' I started towards the huge craft and, as I entered, I was amazed to see it was larger on the inside than it was on the outside.

"Next, I was lying naked on a black table across from another naked man. There were no restraints, but there was something like an electrical force that held me in place. I could not see very far in the craft because the light acted funny—there was light but it did not spread or disperse. The guy next to me told me his name was Tommy and that he came from the other side of the park and was twenty years old. He had copper-red hair and, like me, he was not fully under their spell, so to say, inasmuch as he did not just go along with the Saurians like everyone else did with a glazed look in their eyes. He was cussing the dark figures that were moving up and down between us. He was yelling at them to leave me alone, telling them, 'He's just a kid, you bastards! He's just a kid.' I could not move and felt as if there was a magnet holding me to the black, smooth, plastic-like table. I could only turn my head, and that was how I saw him. There was a group of these shadowy, robed figures working on him too. They paid neither him nor me any attention but just went on with their work. I asked the man, 'Is everyone out here?' And he said, 'All those on this side of Third Avenue.' I was told that there were many others being taken, but they were brought to a different location. Tommy then said, 'Don't talk to them . . . don't listen to them . . . cuss them . . . fight them . . . never give in to them!'

"I asked one of the beings why their ship looked bigger inside than outside and was told that we were not actually in the ship, but in a kind of pocket that they generated and that's why the lights behaved the way they did. I was told that they did not always use a craft to travel; sometimes they used pockets. This is what the Saurian meant the night before by shifting dimensions. The next thing that I knew, I was waking up in bed again and because I found myself in bed in my home afterwards, I was told by my mother it meant they were 'dreams.'"

Many of my readers have read and seen the stories of alien abductions in books and on television about the "grays" that physically take people aboard a spacecraft of some sort and perform medical procedures on them, but Posey's experience was something different. Many believe that human beings are spiritual beings in a physical body. If that is true, then the spirit or astral body can be taken out of the physical body and taken by beings that are interdimensional. This is a frightening thought, since millions of people around the world can be taken out of their bedrooms while they sleep by these interdimensional beings and experimented on or programmed with information in some way and then placed once again in their bedrooms, back in their bodies, thinking after they awake that it was only a dream.

Posey's experiences took place just outside New York City in a very populated area, and he saw everyone in the neighborhood going into the ship. When people wake up after they have been returned, they may think that it was just a dream and in time forget about it. Some individuals may never remember anything, but they may experience a strange feeling when they wake. Perhaps people with psychic abilities remember a great deal more, and they can't be placed fully under the "spell" of these interdimensional creatures. Since the number of people in the world who have kinetic psychic abilities is considerably less when compared to those whose abilities are dormant, the number of individuals remembering an incident like this is very small. Posey no doubt is a psychic, and since childhood he has had contact with a number of different types of beings from another dimension.

SEVEN

ANGELS, JINN, AND EXTRATERRESTRIALS

An ancient legend in the Qur'an (the Koran) says that God (Allah) created the physical beings of the universe from matter; he created the jinn from smokeless fire and the angels from light. Modern science considers this legend to be nothing more than a fairy tale taken from a number of mythological beliefs. However, if you take a close look at the "fairy tale," it makes sense. There is no doubt in my mind that a multitude of different types of intelligent beings exist in the cosmos, and who is to say they all have physical bodies? The intelligent beings behind much of the UFO-contact experience represent human encounters with a number of different types of living intelligent beings having different forms. The following is a case taken from my files that documents an encounter with each type of being.

BEINGS OF MATTER

The physical beings seem to be the extraterrestrials who are dependent upon a technology that allows them to traverse the universe. These physical beings are the "grays," both large and small. There are different types of beings reported in a classic ET encounter, and they all seem to be restricted by the physical laws of time and space. These beings most likely come from a number of nearby star systems and may have been studying the development of life on Earth for thousands of centuries. They are responsible for abductions of human beings and performing what seems to be genetic experiments.

Human beings, animals, and plants belong to this classification of living creatures in the physical universe since we are all made of complex molecules and need to take in other forms of matter to maintain our bodies. Most likely the universe is teeming with life, and the technology levels and wisdom of many of our neighbors in the cosmos are not on the same level. Some races, the older ones, could be more advanced and may be responsible for overlooking what takes place in the physical universe. They may also be responsible for keeping an eye on developing races like us and watching the direction that we might take toward enlightenment or self-destruction.

A CLASSIC ET ENCOUNTER

The following encounter with a physical ET took place during July of 2002 in the town of Putnam Valley, New York. It involves three young men, ages twenty, twenty-five, and twenty-eight. When I interviewed each of them, their stories were pretty much the same. Each did have a slightly different experience during their abduction, however. I have included the testimony of the oldest, whose name is Robert. This is his story as told to me in December of 2002.

"I was camping with my friends Frank and Chuck in the Taconic area just outside Fahnestock State Park, which is located in the Putnam Valley–Kent Cliffs area. We found a good campsite away from the main park area on top of a hill overlooking the valley, and the view of the area and sky was breathtaking. We spent the day hiking, and when we made it back to the camp it was starting to get dark. It was now about 8:30 p.m. on July 22, and the weather was mostly clear with a few puffy cumulus clouds hanging in the sky. When we looked out to the valley and the sky above from our location, it couldn't have been more beautiful in a painting. We rolled out our sleeping bags and made a small fire and ate our dinner. We knew that the area was famous for UFO sightings and even though none of us had ever had a sighting, we were open-minded about them being real and even joked about seeing one.

"As the sun set, I talked about UFOs, but I could tell by the faces of Frank and Chuck that the thought did scare them a little, so I decided not to tell any more campfire 'ghost stories' that night. We retired about eleven or so and put out the fire, and soon after that Frank said, 'Do you hear that?'

Chuck and I woke up and heard this low-frequency buzzing sound, which seemed to be coming from the woods. Frank pointed up to the sky and said, 'What's that?' I looked up and saw this bright star-like thing just above us flashing from red to green and blue then back again to red. All three of us stood up and watched it, then it seemed to get lower and lower in the sky. We jumped into the nearby brush for cover, and this thing came down to about fifty feet above our heads. It was more than one light, it was a triangle-shaped dark object with rows of red, green, white and blue lights on it that were flashing up and down. The buzzing sound was so loud now that we had to hold our hands over our ears, but the strange thing was, the noise seemed to be coming from the woods, not from the UFO. I call it a UFO because what else could it have been? I certainly could not identify it.

"Then the UFO turned like it was on a wheel and drifted over our heads to a clearing on the other side of the hill. As it passed over, I could tell that it was made of some type of dark metal and although it was massive, at least seventy-five feet long, it hung above us like it was a balloon. Well, we lost the object behind a number of trees, but could tell it was there because the trees were now illuminated with a bright white light. We walked over to that area, and when we came to a clearing, we saw the UFO just above the trees projecting down a brilliant beam of white light. We were only about two hundred feet away, and under the beam illuminated by the light were these strange people. We could make out at least ten figures, three of them were tall and very thin, while the rest of them were short, stubby, and looked like fat little children running around. I don't know what they were doing, but what was to happen next would change me forever.

"As we were looking at the 'people' under the object, one of the tall beings started raising his arms and moving his hands around in our direction as if he was trying to signal us. Then a flash of light came from this tall creature and it hit us, and when it did, it felt like a bolt of lightning and we were all knocked down to the ground. We were still conscious and could talk to each other, but we could not move our arms and legs. Then all of a sudden these creatures were all around us, lifting us to our feet and carrying us. This was a scary thing, since we could not move and these 'aliens' were taking us to the light under the ship. The 'aliens' were about half my size (about three feet), and there were at least twenty of them, five holding each of us and the rest leading the way (fig. 17, alien beings reported in Hudson Valley, New York). They had some type of device in their hands that looked like a glowing yellow wand, and when they waved it the shrubs and bushes would flatten down so that they could walk through them.

"We then arrived at the hill and there was one tall alien there. He looked like the smaller ones, but was very slim and had lighter skin. The small guys had huge heads, dark gray skin, and their eyes were big and round. They reminded me of cartoon characters. I could not see a mouth or ears, and they were wearing these tight, black one-piece outfits with some type of insignia on their right chest, which looked like a four with a line going through it. The tall being was over seven feet tall and was so skinny he looked like he would

Figure 17. Drawing of aliens seen in Hudson Valley area of
New York from 1982 to 1995.

fall over at any time. His arms and legs were very long and
his skin was a very light gray. His fingers were long and he
only had three on each hand. The tall guy then made a circular motion with his hand, and all of a sudden we were in
this bright light, so bright it was blinding, but I could tell we
were moving and going upward. The next thing I remember,
I am lying down on a black table that felt like plastic. I was
not restrained, but I can't move my arms and legs. I could
move my head and eyes just enough to see around the room.
The room I was in was barely lit with a gray-like light, and
I could see that there were at least ten other tables all in a
circle.

"The distance between each table was about eight feet or so. I could see Frank and Chuck on each side of me, but they seemed to be sleeping. Across the room I could barely see the images of other people on the tables, but I could not tell if they were men or women. All the time there was this buzzing and clicking noise that almost sounded like there were insects in the room. I laid there for several moments and got really scared, thinking maybe this was some type of extraterrestrial alien biology class and we were the lesson of the day: human dissection!

"All of a sudden, a door appeared across the room and the aliens that took us from the woods came in. There were about seven of them with one big skinny guy. The little ones divided up and went to the tables and seemed to be working on the people with some type of instruments. Several of them came over to the tables that Chuck and Frank were on and it looked like they were sticking a needle in their eyes, and then into their stomach area. When they pulled out the needle they placed something that looked like blood in a test tube filled with a glowing yellow liquid. I thought for sure they were going to do me next. At least the others were asleep, but I was awake.

"Then the tall, skinny alien guy came over and smiled at me and put his hand on the top of my head. He talked to me using some type of device that he held near his throat. He told me that I would not be harmed and although they regretted taking me and my companions, they had no choice, they do this to help save their race. He told me that they needed fresh DNA to help preserve their kind, since for a very long time they reproduced by copying each other and making clone-like beings, but now since they have done it for such a long time the copying procedure is breaking down. He said you can only make a copy from a copy so many times before it fades—that I understood. He said that a long time ago his race searched this section of the galaxy, looking for life forms that were compatible to them that would not be rejected when the DNA from both races was combined. He said we are the only beings in the galaxy that they have found that can combine with them to save their race. He told me they were from a star system thirty light years from Earth and that they travel through tunnels in space to get to here in a short time.

"The being then said to me that they did not put me to sleep because there was something in my brain put there by another race that made it dangerous to do so. He also said that they will not use my DNA for the same reason. I didn't understand this, and when I asked the alien, who was without doubt the leader of the group, he would not give me any more information because he said it would be better if I didn't know what the 'others' did to me. The next thing I remember, I am in the woods at the camp, sitting, and Frank and Chuck are with me in their sleeping bags fast asleep. I thought at first it was a dream, but when Frank and Chuck told of the same dream, I broke out in a cold sweat. They remember the point where we saw the aliens under the craft illuminated by the light; they do not remember being taken inside the craft. When I told them what else took place, they started crying and shaking their heads, saying, 'No way, no way!'

"It was dawn, and we packed up our bags and left and never went back. For weeks afterwards we all had dreams of the UFO and the beings that abducted us. To them that part was just a dream, but to me it was real. Since that time, I have not had another encounter with the beings or even a sighting, but for some reason I can't explain, I just feel different, like I have been taken apart and put back together, wrong."

Although Frank and Chuck have no conscious recollection of the actual abduction, they know something happened to them that night after they saw the aliens under the object in the woods. To this day they would rather forget about it and will not watch any UFO specials on TV or read any UFO books. However, Robert has become very interested in finding out more and is anxious to talk to other people who had a similar experience. If you would like to correspond with Robert, you can get his e-mail by contacting me at the e-mail or address at the end of the this book.

BEINGS OF SMOKELESS FIRE

The second class of living beings reported in contact/UFO encounters is the jinn. Most people have never heard of the word *jinn*, or *djinn*, but know the word *genie*, which is a common name that has been made popular in the movies, on television, and in some classic books like *The Arabian Nights*. The jinn are said to be made from smokeless fire, which really means plasma, the fourth state of matter. Although the jinn appear in a physical form, they can take on a number of different shapes and have the ability to rearrange matter into different substances. They can also manipulate energy and matter, but their power in this area seems to be limited.

The jinn exist between the universe of light and matter, and according to legend the entire race was placed there by the angels because of things they did that upset the balance of the universe. In the legends of many cultures, the jinn are called the con men of creation since they will do whatever it takes to come into the physical universe where they will be all-powerful and delight in a multitude of physical pleasures. The Native Americans, as well as other tribal cultures, called them the great tricksters, and it was considered to be very dangerous for an individual to open communication with them. In the Islamic belief they are called *jinn, djinn, aamar, arwaah, shaitan, shayateen, genie,* and *afreet.* Jinn are classified according to their spiritual awareness and technology. Some of the jinn seem to be docile and want no connection with the physical universe, while others are just plain nasty and will do whatever they have to for the fulfillment of their goals and desires.

Over the many years of my research into the channeling craze and other types of paranormal phenomena, I have come to the conclusion that over 95 percent of all authentic channeling is done by the jinn. This is actually a low number, since I consider 87 percent of all people who claim to channel ETs or other beings (based on my research from field investigations) to be charlatans and unstable individuals, but some I believe are authentic and channeling something more than their own imaginations. When channeling, the jinn will take the identity of an extraterrestrial (like Monka, mentioned earlier) or an angel and sometimes even come through as a loved one who has passed over. Whatever the person channeling is expecting or believes, the jinn will take on that form and identity. The jinn seem to want to use the "channel" and the other people who attend to draw energy to establish a foothold in our dimension. Jinn are an order of beings separate from humans and angels, and we have very little understanding of them because they stay hidden from us. The jinn are without a doubt the intelligence behind many paranormal events that have been recorded over the years and are responsible for part of the UFO experience, especially in the form of psychic contact. The word *jinn* is Arabic; it translates into English as meaning "hidden," and this is what they appear to want to do, stay hidden and cover up their true identity.

JUST WHO ARE THE JINN?

According to ancient Islamic stories, the jinn have free will and many of them, when compared to human beings, have great power. They can appear as human while others can take the forms of strange creatures, which, by the way, are often reported in the paranormal area of study called cryptozoology. Writer and paranormal researcher John Keel (famous for the book and movie *The Mothman Prophecies*), in his book *UFOs: Operation Trojan Horse*, is the first to identify the cause of many UFO encounters as being the result of creatures from another dimension. It must be understood that we share our planet with a great multitude of unseen beings. Once you identify the role of the jinn, the high strangeness parts of the UFO phenomenon like channeling, Bigfoot,

Mothman, poltergeists, and the so-called ascended masters who communicate through certain psychics become clear.

The jinn in their normal form look like they are half human and half reptile. Originally they were thought to be spirits of nature who often played tricks on susceptible humans. According to the Islamic belief, the jinn can be agents of good and evil (just like every other living being in the universe); however, most are evil and enjoy punishing humans because they feel that God placed humankind in a better dimension. In ancient times, accidents, disease, and untimely deaths were thought to be the result of a wrathful jinn.

The jinn can only enter our dimension through a human conduit or host, most likely a person who has active or dormant psychic abilities. The jinn are said to possess the power to heal, change shape, control the elements of nature, create illusions, and control the minds of people who accept them. This is why the jinn, when channeling through a human host, will often identify themselves as extraterrestrials, angels, or loved ones who have died to get the confidence of the people in the channeling session.

A JINN ENCOUNTER

The story that I am about to relate to you is so bizarre that I often have to re-examine the case material to ensure that it really happened. Every time I tell this story I still get goose bumps, and the hair on the back of my neck stands up. This is the first time that I am writing about this bizarre case, which at first I thought was just a typical UFO abduction involving a family who, for several generations, has had contact with some type of nonhuman intelligence. The case study began in 1978; however, it wasn't until the turn of the new millennium that I finally accepted the fact that it wasn't the ETs that were involved, but the jinn at their worst.

THE DREAM TEAM

During my early years of UFO research, sometime in the mid-seventies, I was somewhat naive of what the UFO phenomenon represented and had no idea of how really complex it was. I did firmly believe that many sightings were the result of misinterpretations of conventional objects and bright planets, but I also kept an open mind about the possibility that some sightings could be extraterrestrial in origin, other beings visiting planet Earth for exploratory and scientific purposes.

There were other cases that came to my attention that involved more than a sighting or a close encounter with a strange object; these cases were of actual contact and paranormal phenomena. During that time, I interviewed a number of people who said they had seen visions, contended that they had been teleported to other worlds, and made claims of contact with beings from another world or dimension. It was my policy to avoid these cases since when I met with the individuals, they had no proof, just a fantastic story. At the time I was looking for photographs, video, and physical traces that would document the existence of UFOs.

During those early years, I worked with a number of researchers and together we set out to explore uncharted territory by documenting the UFO experience. This team consisted of six people: Dave, a biologist; Thomas, a police officer; Jake, an engineer; Carl, a corporate executive; Frank, a commercial airline pilot; and myself, who at that time had just received a degree in astronomy from the University of Texas, so I guess you can say that I was the resident astronomer for the group. Our research group was well balanced from many disciplines, and together we investigated and cataloged dozens of UFO cases. We were the Dream Team of those early days of UFOl-ogy. However, we were all put to the test both mentally and physically when we were asked to investigate a case that involved a family that had a history going back at least three generations of UFO sightings, abductions, and contact with a malevolent intelligence that was not of this universe.

THE GLOBES OF LIGHT

During the month of February of 1978, I received a call from a thirty-five-year-old single mother who will be referred to as Sandra. Sandra told me that she, her mother, and her daughter had had many encounters with UFOs and had seen alien beings. She told me on the phone that alien-like beings had walked through the walls into their home through a black rotating hole on numerous occasions and had taken them away to a place they can't remember, since after they would walk through the "hole," they would black out. It seems that this was going on since Sandra's mother was nine years old, and she also recalls times when she was a child going through the "black hole." She then told me that it stopped for many years, and it started up once again with Sandra's daughter Kathy being the focus of attention. I called the team and gave them the background into the case. They all were anxious to go and visit this person since the number of abduction cases available at that time was few.

We arrived at Sandra's home in Cold Springs, New York, on the evening of February 16, 1978. The weather was warm for that time of the year, with a light mist in the air. After the normal formalities, I asked about her experiences. Sandra told us that she had many sightings of UFOs when she was a child, but most of what she saw as an adult were balls of lights that followed her car and came into her home. She said that on one occasion a blue ball of light came into her home through the living room window, and as it did, the television and lights all went out, only to go back on again when the object disappeared through the ceiling. She then said that on several occasions, the globes of light would follow her while she drove home, whether it was day or night. As we sat in her modest living room, her daughter Kathy, then ten at the time, pointed to the window and said, "UFO out there." We all ran to the window and then opened the door and witnessed a yellow globe of light about six inches or so in diameter move across the front lawn about fifty feet from the house. The light was about ten feet or so above the ground and seemed to be wobbling as it moved from right to left.

I walked out the door, trying to get closer to the light with the hope of getting a better look at it, while my partners were flashing their cameras. As I got to within twenty feet of it, I felt a tingling up and down my neck, as if there were static electricity in the air. The light then stopped in midair as if observing me and then shot straight up into the sky.

Needless to say, when I returned to the house we were quite excited and although Dave, the biologist, had seen a UFO a number of years before, this was the first sighting for the rest of us. We all sat once again in the living room and Sandra began to tell us how the "space people" came and got them and how they didn't remember where they went since they would wake up in their beds. She told us that the space people looked like the statues of some of the gargoyles she has seen on top of old buildings and in pictures on some of the churches in Europe. She said that when they are taken, the "aliens" do not say anything, and they seem powerless to resist. Sandra also told us that her daughter Kathy would talk to them during the day and night, and at times, as if in a trance, she would say something like, "We want to come into your world, work with us and we will reward you." Despite our questioning, Sandra insisted that she knew that this was not her daughter talking.

This aspect of the case was getting a little strange for me and the others, so we talked Sandra into allowing us to bring a psychologist next time who was trained in regression hypnosis. Sandra eagerly agreed, since she wanted to get to the bottom of the strange things that have been happening to her family over the past years, so a date was set for March 15. Sandra gave us her mother's number to see if she could add to the experiences, but when contacted, although she admitted to having a multitude of encounters with UFOs and "aliens," she preferred not to comment about them and said she would like to forget about them, since the experiences stopped when she reached middle age. Sandra's mother was actually afraid that if the topic were brought up again that the "aliens" would come back for her.

SANDRA'S HYPNOSIS SESSION

The therapist, Dr. Merger, was a good friend of mine whom I had worked with several times in the past. He insisted that only one member of our team be present at the session with him, and I was elected. On March 15, at about 2:00 p.m., we arrived for the regressive hypnosis session at Sandra's home. Sandra's daughter was sleeping at the time in her bedroom and was ill with the flu. It was my usual procedure to tape the sessions so that information could be recalled. I would also take notes, and it's a good thing that I did, since something very strange happened to the tape recordings of that session. However, before I get into that part, let me relate to you Sandra's experience under hypnosis.

It took quite a long time, perhaps a half-hour or so, before she relaxed and went "under." She started by relating a sighting that she and her daughter had in 1976 where she was awakened at about midnight by a buzzing sound that seemed to be vibrating through the house. She got out of bed and walked into the living room to find her daughter walking around in circles, saying, "The people from the hole are here, the people from the hole are here." She said that her daughter seemed to be in a trance, and she had to grab her by the shoulders and shake her to get her out of it. She still heard the noise and walked outside to the deck and saw a red object in the sky that looked like a blur. As she watched, the red blur changed from a circle to an oblong shape or an ellipse.

At that moment, she regressed to a time when she was a child and woke up in the early hours of the morning to find three beings with leather-like skin standing over her bed, smiling at her. She was only five at the time, and they told her that they would not hurt her because they needed people like her to work with. She then saw a spinning black hole appear and the beings were "sucked" into it with a sound like a vacuum picking up a large object and getting clogged. At this point she started breathing heavily, and Dr. Merger had to calm her down, because the experience as a child was too traumatic for her to handle.

The next experience she remembered was a night in the winter of 1977 where she and her daughter were sleeping together in the same bed. Sandra often did this since she was afraid that the "beings from the hole" would take her daughter and not return her. She remembers waking up at two or three in the morning to see a figure standing at the foot of the bed. The "man" was about six feet tall and dressed in something like a monk's robe with a hood over his head. He then pulled the hood off his head and she gasped in fear because he looked like the devil, with long ears and a pointed nose. His skin was like leather and there seemed to be a blue glow illuminating the room. The being pointed to her daughter, and when he did this, she put her arms around young Kathy because she thought he wanted to take her. He said in a hoarse, deep voice, "I need you to come with me and in return I will give you whatever you desire." She yelled at the creature and said, "No way! Get out of here!" and started praying to God and the angels for help. The being then looked angry and said, "God has no power here. I will come for you when I am ready." The creature then vanished through a swirling black hole that appeared on the right side of the wall. Sandra slept with the lights on every night after that, and the same being would make at least three more appearances over the next two months during the day and night and would make the same request. With each appearance, she said no to the creature and prayed and each time it looked angry and vanished.

At this point Sandra became very agitated, her pulse was at 130 and she was breathing rapidly and shallowly, with sweat pouring down her face. Dr. Merger decided it was time to wake her and make her forget what she had related under hypnosis. As soon as Sandra woke up, she got up and ran to her daughter Kathy's room. Before she reached the room, Kathy started screaming and jumped out of bed. She met her mother in the hall and held on to her and said, "The man from the hole came and said he was going to take me." Her mother tried to tell her it was only a dream, and when Sandra asked her what else the man said, she pointed to me and said, "The man said that he would get him and his friends if they don't leave us alone." Well, that sent chills up and down my spine—this child was scared half to death and I could feel the tension and a presence in the house that I could only classify as evil.

I then went back to the living room and retrieved my tape recorder and notes, since I was meeting the next day with the members of the team to go over Dr. Merger's session with Sandra and to update them on many of the events that had taken place. We stayed about a half-hour longer, then said our goodbyes and told Sandra that we would be in touch.

THE VOICE ON THE TAPE

The next evening we all met in my basement and I went over what took place that night during the regressive hypnosis session with Sandra. I went over my notes and told the group I had not listened to the tape yet and needed to rewind the cassette. I began to play the tape, and we could hear Dr. Merger slowly relaxing Sandra, but what was to happen next shocked the group and would change their lives forever. As soon as she started recalling the events and details of the beings she encountered, the voices of Dr. Merger and Sandra faded and in its place came what sounded like a pulsing siren or high-pitched electrical noise. Then all we heard was howling, screaming, and what sounded like animal sounds with an overtone of some strange language. Everyone in the room including myself just looked at the tape player with a blank stare. *What the hell is this?* I thought. Jake, the engineer, said that it sounded like something from *The Exorcist* movie and although he was an atheist and didn't believe in the devil, if the devil did exist, Jake said, this is what he would sound like.

The tape was covered with these sounds from almost the beginning to end, but in the background, very faintly, you could hear Sandra and Dr. Merger. We continued to listen, and then a very audible voice was heard on the tape, and in perfect English it said, "Stop playing with my head, they pointed you out to us and we know where and how to get you all." That was enough to scare even the bravest paranormal researcher. We were all very young and new at the game, and UFO research was more like a hobby to us, but now because of this, it became a terrifying reality. The intelligence responsible for Sandra's and her daughter's encounters wanted to stay hidden, and the message was clear: *Back off!*

I took the tape to a friend of mine who did audio recordings for the State University of New York at Purchase. He listened to the tape and thought someone was trying to play a joke on us. I assured him that the tape was new and never left my custody from the time of the recording to the time of playing it for the group. There was a very short time when I walked down the hall to Kathy's room when she began screaming about the man from the black hole, but the recorder was only ten or so feet away from me. I asked my friend what the language sounded like to him and he said, "It sounds like English." I replied, "English?" He then said, "Yes, English backwards." He knew this because he often rewound tapes with the audio on and heard the material he was working on, such as music, singing, and lectures done on campus, backwards. He then took the tape and ran it backwards through his console, and he was right, it was English, but backwards! Although we could not understand a section of the tape due to the howling and electrical-like noises that were present, there was a part that was very audible, and it was clear that whoever or whatever put the message on the tape wanted us to hear it and, in my opinion, wanted to frighten us away. The following is a brief transcript of some of the things the voice said on the tape.

THE MESSAGE OF ABLIS

"I am Ablis [?], supreme commander of the Millennia Council. We come from a place that is parallel with your world. We once lived in your world in the light like you but were placed here before your recorded history so that you may live in a world that was once ours. Because of experiments that went wrong, our race was shifted into this dimension where there are no physical pleasures. We are trying to enter your world once again but need humans who have a sensitive spirit [psychics?] to act as a connection to our existence so that we may enter yours. The holes that are talked about are portals. We can make them appear or use natural ones as in the location you call the Bermuda Triangle. People who disappear on your planet fall into these voids or we take them to serve our means. The holes are the only way that we can communicate with this planet. Those who enter our world are not dead, but they are in a timeless void. If you continue to interfere with our work [the voice begins to slow down and fade as if running out of energy], we will have no choice but to take action against you."

When the recording was played for the team, it caused a great deal of anxiety. The tone of the voice convinced everyone present that whoever this Ablis was, he meant business. The name Ablis was hard to make out on the tape, and it could have been Iblis. Iblis is the name of an evil being from the Qur'an, and he is considered to be the leader of the al-Shairan or Satan, those beings that revolted against the will of God. According to legend, Iblis was the leader of a group of jinn who was made of fire, and because he refused when

Durango Public Library

Items that you checked out

Title: Fahrenheit 451
ID: 10500053685547
Due: Monday, June 3, 2024

Title: Interdimensional universe : the new science of ufos, paranormal phenomena & otherdimensional beings
ID: 10500038916646
Due: Monday, June 3, 2024

Title: Paranormal : my life in pursuit of the afterlife
ID: 10500043222242
Due: Monday, June 3, 2024

Title: The darkest places : unsolved mysteries, true crimes, and harrowing disasters in the wild
ID: 10500051216607
Due: Monday, June 3, 2024

Title: The Godmother : murder, vengeance, and the bloody struggle of Mafia women
ID: 10500053680039
Due: Monday, June 3, 2024

Title: The handy psychology answer book
ID: 10500045568822
Due: Monday, June 3, 2024

Title: The Martian chronicles
ID: 10500054091447
Due: Monday, June 3, 2024

Total items: 7
Account balance: $0.00
5/13/2024 1:20 PM
Checked out: 7
Overdue: 0
Hold requests: 0
Ready for pickup: 0

Have a nice day!

ordered by God to bow down and give up his place to Adam (mankind), he and his followers were cast out of this world into a void. Iblis's goal is the destruction of the human race by tempting people with material things to pull them away from God (the wishes of the genie). Well, this sounds quite a bit like what the voice said on the tape, and although I've had this information since 1978, I really didn't put it all together until 2002, when I began extensive research on angels and jinn and the connection with the UFO experience. I also did further research on the name Iblis and compared it to other names that appeared in religious writings, UFO channeling, and other forms of contacts. I was not surprised to find a host of names like Ashtar, Aphax, Iblis, Ablis, Eblis, Shatam, and Ibis whose origins predate Islam and Christianity.

THE EXPERIMENT

In 1978, I could not accept the idea that there were malevolent creatures in the universe trying to take advantage of lesser beings for their own purpose. Unlike several members of the team, I wasn't ready to accept that the voice and sounds were put on the tape by supernatural means. I became aware that other UFO investigators, while taping the statements of witnesses, also got sounds on their tape, including distorted voices, music, and other unusual sounds. Recording heads and players operate on the principle of magnetic resonance. There is a very thin coating of magnetic iron material on the plastic tape, and with the use of a magnet or electromagnetic pulse, sounds are recorded. Therefore, you don't need magic

to place a sound on the tape that is not audible in the room—
it can also be done by an electromagnetic wave or pulse.

Having some background in radio and physics, I decided
to perform an experiment. At the time, I was an amateur
radio operator and had considerable equipment. I took an
old citizens band radio (CB) and tuned it so it would be off
frequency in both the upper and lower sidebands. At first I
used only a transmitting power of 4 watts, and I was able to
produce an off-frequency signal than spanned a considerable
area of the 11-meter band. In the next room, I placed a cassette recorder in the record mode. I began talking into the
transceiver (CB radio) microphone with the hope of being
able to put something on the cassette recorder. I went into
the room and played the tape and there was nothing. I tried
the experiment again and this time, to ensure that I wasn't
picking up an audible sound, I disconnected the built-in microphone on the recorder. I went back to the CB radio and
transmitted on a number of frequencies, and although my
voice was coming across on the TV (and most likely those of
many of the neighbors on the street), there was still nothing
on the cassette recorder.

I decided to try the experiment once again, but this time
increasing the power using a linear amplifier. This device
would boost my transmitting power from 4 watts to 750
watts. According to the regulations of the Federal Communications Commission (FCC), it was illegal to transmit this
much power on the CB band, especially with a radio that was
purposely made to operate "out of tune." However, I proceeded with the experiment because the amount of time I

would be transmitting would be short. I then transmitted a signal and talked, sang a rock and roll song, and played music for five minutes. There was no doubt that I was knocking out the reception of every television set on the street, and you must remember this was a time before cable, so people were receiving the TV stations with antennas on the roof. I went back to the recorder, rewound it, and to my delight, when I played it my voice, the music, and everything I transmitted was on the tape. However, the sounds and my voice were distorted, and it did sound like the tape from Sandra's hypnotic session in which Ablis or Iblis sent us a message.

I was actually able to place my voice on the recorder using the extra power and transmitter as far as 310 feet from the antenna! Who or whatever put the voice on the tape was using methods that are explainable by the laws of physics; it wasn't any type of supernatural magic. I began to suspect a hoax, since if someone was involved who had even a basic knowledge of radio, they could accomplish the same thing and be responsible for putting the voice and other sounds on the tape that night by transmitting a signal from a house nearby.

The talking backwards in English could have been accomplished before transmission by taping a message then re-recording it, then playing it backwards. The next day I took a drive around Sandra's neighborhood, looking for amateur (ham) radio or CB antennas on the roofs of houses, and I found three that were in range that could be responsible. Since I had a radio in the car, I actually talked with two of radio operators while they were on the air and met with them at their homes to compare equipment. This was customary and a common practice in those days when ham and CB radio were very popular. After I looked at their equipment, it was clear that neither of the individuals could have produced the voice on the tape, and they didn't seem to know Sandra and her daughter personally. At that point, I thought a hoax was unlikely, but I didn't rule it out. When I called each of the members of the team and told them of my findings, they seemed interested, but distant. It was clear that something else was going on with each of them, events that were causing severe problems in their personal lives.

THE ATTACK OF 1978

I didn't hear from any of the team members for a week. I thought for sure they would be interested in the results of my experiment that showed the voice on the tape could be explained within the confines of the laws of physics. A few days later, I received a strange call from Dave, the biologist. He informed me that he had started hearing voices at night and then the voices increased in frequency and he heard them in the day. He told me that it sounded like someone was right up to his ears (on both sides of his head) trying to tell him something. He knew they wanted something from him, but he didn't know what. I really didn't know how to take this at the time, so I tried to discuss it with him to see if there was a physical or even psychological cause for the voices that he heard. The next day he called me once again to inform me that he made contact with the beings who were whispering in his ears and that they were extraterrestrial. He told me that three of them appeared in his bedroom and that they were dark blue and about four to five feet tall with red eyes. Once again this type of an experience was all new to me, and I just listened silently as he described his night visitation. Dave said he woke up at three in the morning and saw the beings standing in a circle around his bed. They were talking but he could not understand them. Then he closed his eyes and they were gone.

After that conversation, I didn't hear from Dave for several days, and when I tried to call his home there was no answer. One week later I received a call from a relative who informed me that Dave had jumped in front of a train and was killed! After a few days of investigation the police closed the case and ruled it as a suicide. I could not accept this since I knew Dave to be one of the most intelligent and grounded persons that I have ever met, and until this day his death remains a mystery to me.

Shortly after Dave's death, Frank (the pilot) called me and said he was paid a visit by a man in a dark suit who identified himself as an agent of the National Security Agency. Frank said that the man told him that UFOs were a matter of national security and that if he didn't give up his own investigations, he would lose his commercial pilot's license and not be allowed to fly for any airline for the rest of his life. Frank told me he was out of the group because he didn't want to "mess" with the government, since he had a family to support. This was the last I would hear from him. As time went on, the team started falling apart, with each member in some way being scared out of the field of UFO–paranormal research by some unseen force.

I decided to try and reach the other members of our group to see what was going on, and after leaving several messages, I finally was able to reach Carl (the corporate executive). We talked for a while about what had taken place with the other members of the team, and then he told me about a "dream" he had the night before. Carl said that in the "dream," he woke up in the middle of the night and saw a figure standing at the side of the bed. The being he saw was tall and had a hood over his head and some type of loose-fitting robe and was surrounded by a soft, pale-green light. Carl then sat up in the bed and was so scared he didn't notice if his wife was by his side. The entity then stretched out his hand and in it was a glowing-red, beating heart. The entity then said, "This could be your heart" and then squeezed it, causing it to burst, spraying blood through the air, on Carl, the walls, and the bed. Carl said that then he woke in a cold sweat, realized it was just a dream, and saw his wife quietly sleeping. I asked Carl, "Are you sure it was a dream and not some type of telepathic message?" He replied, "I hope it was a dream, and I'm going to leave it at that."

A week or so passed and I didn't hear from Carl, so I called his home and talked to his wife. She informed me that Carl went to the doctor for his routine physical, and they found something wrong with a valve in his heart—he was in the hospital, planning to have surgery. She told me that the doctors expected a full recovery after a two-week stay. Before the surgery, I visited Carl and he seemed to be in good spirits and was not worried, since his surgeon assured him that his condition was an easy one to correct. Three days after the surgery, Carl died from heart failure and the doctors never gave his wife a satisfactory answer why.

This left me, Jake (the engineer), and Thomas (the police officer) as the only ones left in the group. Thomas dropped out of UFO research after having a number of sightings with his wife that terrified both of them. However, Jake continued his own investigations for about a year or so, keeping mostly to himself. I kept in limited contact with him and our last conversation was in 1979 or 1980, when he told me that he was giving up UFO research because he was convinced that the "devil" was behind it all. I found this very surprising from a man who at one time professed to be a dedicated atheist. It seems that Jake had so many bizarre things happen to him that he was beginning to live his life in fear. He claimed on numerous occasions that he was being followed by black helicopters and that he had a number of very close encounters at night with UFOs—so close and frequent were his encounters that he became fearful of going out at night. Jake also claimed he was experiencing poltergeist phenomena in his home and told me that he was sure his son (twelve at the time) was being possessed by some sort of "demon."

Driven by his fear, Jake became a born-again Christian, and a short time later I lost contact with him. I do know that he started preaching on the grounds of a number of colleges in Connecticut and New York, warning people about the connection between the devil and UFOs. In 1981, a relative of mine brought a newspaper article to my attention in which Jake was arrested for burning UFO books on the lawn of the University of Connecticut near Hartford. With this last bit of news, the once Dream Team was no more, and I remained the only one of that group who today is still actively involved in UFO research.

I must make it clear that during that time nothing much happened to me and in the years to follow I would continue to investigate the claims of individuals who say they encountered strange beings. Recently I looked over many of my past cases and realized quite a number of them were most likely jinn encounters. This is one of the reasons why I caution people who channel angels, spirits, or the "space people."

BEINGS OF LIGHT

The third type of living being that appears in many UFO contacts is the angelic-like beings. They are reported to be able to take on physical form; however, their original appearance is of a glowing orb or column of light. When contact is made with humans, they take the shape of a humanoid and although the reports vary, the majority of cases describe them as being very tall (six to seven feet) and slim, with very pale white skin and flowing, long blonde, platinum, or copper-red hair and blue or green eyes. In UFO literature, they are referred to as the "Nords," since they look like someone who could be from Norway or Sweden. They have the ability to appear and disappear and although they have been associated with some type of disk-like craft, they don't seem to need a vehicle to travel across the cosmos.

The angelic beings do not abduct people; they seem to want to communicate with us and keep our technology and spiritual development on the correct path. As in the case of a Mr. Dean Fagerstrom (who is mentioned in my book *Contact of the 5th Kind*), the angelic beings also inspire a person to write spiritual teachings or on occasion to produce technical diagrams. Mr. Fagerstrom claimed that he was in contact with a number of these beings; they are called Donestra, Kilestra, and Aphax. Like the jinn and the physical beings, there are good angels, bad ones, and those that are indifferent or that couldn't care less about humans.

WHO ARE THE ANGELS?

The word *angel* means "messenger of God," and although their origin is surrounded in mystery, they appear to be the oldest race of beings in the cosmos. Angels are mentioned in a number of religious texts, and their role in the protection of humanity goes back before Christianity. In paintings during the Middle Ages and renaissance period, angels are shown as being very beautiful, and when you look at them it's hard to tell if they are male or female. This is because according to many biblical references, angels are male and female energy in balanced harmony, much like the yin-yang symbol. Remember, angels are not physical beings, so when I say "male and female," it does not mean in the physical sense—their energy essence is both male and female.

Angels are shown with bird-like wings because they were noted by our ancestors as not being bound to the surface of Earth. They are also shown having halos around them, which is no doubt energy or a powerful aura being emitted. Angels are beings of pure energy, and they are locked within the flow of creation. This means that they have to go with the flow of the universe and creation or be thrown out. This is why it is often said that angels do not have a free will. Unlike humans and jinn who can better themselves and grow, angels seem to be at the top of the pyramid; they can be nothing more, and nothing less.

We know that there are evil angels because the Bible tells us that there was a war in heaven where one-third of the heavenly host was cast out. There is also mention in Revelation of a second war between the angels that broke out much later and could still be going on. This would explain the apparent discord of the universe, especially here on tiny planet Earth. Angels work to keep things in balance, making sure that everything from the largest galaxy to the smallest quark at the quantum level flows in harmony with the rest of creation.

FACTS ABOUT ANGELS

Angels are not human and have never been in physical form. So when you leave your physical body, you will not become an angel. Angels have their own type of writing, which is called angelic script, of which there are three types.

The first type of angelic script is made up of symbols that look like modern art. These symbols act as receptors so that a particular angel can channel and direct energy into the physical world. If you want to know how this form of angelic script appears, then take a look at some of the crop circle pictures. Crop circles are quite interesting, since most of them are located over magnetic anomalies. Crop circles are not messages from aliens; they are conduits through which the angelic race enters this world. The physical part of the crop circle is not the conduit; it is formed by magnetic, electromagnetic, and other types of energy that cannot be detected. The plants or crops simply take on the shape that the magnetic field produces, much like sprinkling iron filings on white paper with a magnet under it. The iron filings will show the pattern of the magnetic field produced by the magnet.

The second type of angelic script is a code-like writing that is a combination of ancient Hebrew, Aramaic, and Iberian. This type of script identifies the family or group that an angel belongs to. According to the Bible, this is how God marked the angels to identify them.

The third type of angelic script is an actual writing composed of over 220 characters. These letters and symbols often are written by people who have had contact and who have been shown some type of tablet or book (fig. 18, example of angelic script). Fragments of this form of angelic script also appear in all the written languages of the human race. This form of angelic script could be the root of all written forms of human language. There are many myths that tell how the gods came down from heaven, gave the human race knowledge, and taught them how to express their thoughts in words. Although full sets of this form of angelic script are rare, I have fifteen pages of the symbols, which were obtained from a number of sources, including UFO contactees, psychics, channelers, and ancient writings, and after twenty years I have been able to partially translate it. However, much of the information about the angelic society that is presented in this book is a result of the translation of these symbols.

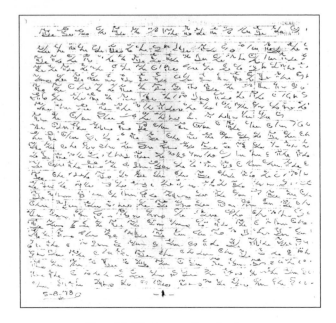

Figure 18. Alien or angelic script done
by Dean Fagerstrom, 1982.

THE ANGELIC SOCIETY

Angels have a structured social order with a group of angels
closer to the physical plane, but most are so far above our
realm of existence that they never interact with physical beings or even jinn. The lower divisions of angels are the groups
that interact with the physical world and belong to three orders. From the lowest to the highest, they are Angels, Archangels, and Principles. The middle division is also divided
into three sections; they are called Authorities, Powers, and
Dominates (or Controllers). Finally, those of the highest or-

der are the Throne angels, Cherubim and Seraphim. Each section and order seems to have billions of these beings of light as their members and are ruled or governed by one powerful angel.

In the religious writings of Christianity, Judaism, and Islam, there are a number of angels mentioned frequently. They are Michael, Gabriel, Raphael, Uzziel, Raguel, and Camael. Personally, I think that angels use vibration energy to identify each other rather than names—each angel has its own energy signature that is unique to that angel, much like a fingerprint or genetic code in human beings. The names of angels were given by human beings to help us relate better to these beings and have a more personal relationship with them. Sometimes the same angel will have several names; this depends on the time in history, culture, and religious belief.

ANGELIC ENCOUNTERS

Encounters with angels go as far back as recorded history, from Abraham and his angelic contacts to the time of Jacob and his wrestling match with the angel Camael. We also can find angelic encounters with the Israelites in Exodus. Angels seemed to have played an important role in the conflict between Moses and Pharaoh. We are told that the angel of death (some say it was Gabriel) took the lives of Egypt's first born. Angels are also mentioned in the New Testament where the angel Gabriel visits Mary to tell her that she was chosen by God to give birth to Jesus. The Prophet Muhammad (570–632) was visited by the angel Gabriel in 610 AD while on retreat at Mount Hira during the month of Ramadan. The archangel dictated the religion of Islam to Muhammad and continued to appear to him several times over a period of twenty-three years.

In 1823, Joseph Smith (1805–1844) said he was visited by an angel named Moroni who told him of an ancient record containing God's true laws. In 1827, the angel channeled this information through him on golden plates resulting in the manuscript *The Book of Mormon*, which was published in 1830. On April 6, 1830, Joseph Smith founded The Church of Jesus Christ of Latter Day Saints and became its first president. Once again a human being claimed contact with an angel and introduced new ideas to the world with the purpose of starting a new religion, this one an offshoot of Christianity.

Today, many psychic mediums and people who channel are also claiming contact with angels. Their apparent goal is to introduce new spiritual ideas to the world from these angelic sources, although none to date have been as successful as Muhammad, Moses, Jesus, and Joseph Smith.

A MODERN–DAY ENCOUNTER

Henry Miller is a soft-spoken man of sixty-four, and if you meet him, you would never guess that he claims to have met "extraterrestrial angels." Although Henry does not look for publicity, after much coaxing he agreed to tell his story to me. The following is Henry's account in his own words.

"Since I was a child of five, this angel would appear right in my bedroom at night and take me to different places where I would meet others like him and people that were also being contacted. His name is Auriel, and he told me that he used to live in the physical universe on a planet called Carium, which is in another galaxy. He said that in the Earth year 1234, he left his physical body and became what he is today: a being of light. He told me the form that he appears in, which is tall with long white hair, green eyes, and very white skin, is the form he likes to take since this is what he looked like when he was 'in the flesh.'

"He said that the people on his planet have evolved to great technological and spiritual lengths and that they lived to be five thousand years old, and when their body can no longer function they become a 'quickening angel,' which means they are in a state between pure energy and the energy of solid matter. He said there are billions like him in the universe, and they travel to different planets to help individuals, but not entire races. He said that to help an entire race deal with war or save them from extinction is beyond his ability and that is left to the ones higher up—what we would call true angels or archangels.

"Now Auriel is male; however, I have seen others in his race that are most definitely female, so like us they have two sexes, but I don't think they reproduce like we do. Auriel would put his hand over my eyes and then I would find myself floating in the air, and he would take me to places that were beautiful with all types of people that looked happy, and the smiles on their faces were so bright they glowed. I asked him over and over to let me stay and not take me home, but he said I had to go back to finish my task in life on planet Earth.

"These visits would take place at least once every other month until I was thirteen, then they stopped. At twenty-one years old, Auriel once again came into my bedroom at an early hour in the morning before sunrise. I was surprised to see him, and when I went to hug him my arms went right through him. He told me that he was a projection and that I was ready to start the communication with him. Then another being appeared, the most beautiful woman I have ever seen. Auriel said her name was Killonia and she was his female part or mate. Unlike Auriel, who had long white hair, she had long bright-red hair and the widest green eyes I have ever seen. She was about his height—I would say six feet or more—and was dressed in a dark green one-piece suit that had stripes on the side. She smiled at me but never spoke a word, but I could tell there was some type of communication going on between them. I guess it was telepathic. Auriel then said I would be contacted again, but he didn't say when and they both just disappeared. Well, the next contact didn't take place until 1999, when I was fifty-five years old.

"I was driving home from work along Route 37 in New Fairfield, Connecticut, listening to the radio. It was a very foggy May night, about 11:00 p.m., and the roads were dark. I came upon a roadblock in the road, and a man walked up to the car and told me to turn left because there is an accident up ahead and I had to take a detour. I turned left, I can't remember the street, and then all of a sudden I hear a voice say, 'Hello Henry.' I looked to the passenger seat and there was Auriel sitting there, smiling. He said, 'I told you I would be back.' I replied, 'But it has been over thirty years!'

He replied by saying something like time has no meaning and although the passage of time seemed long to me, from his perspective the last time we met was only a short time ago.

"He told me that he was going to take me to a ship in space and there I would meet other people and have a procedure done to me that will allow his people to send information through me. All of a sudden the car was lifted off the ground, and the next thing I know I am inside what looked like a big hangar. Auriel was standing next to me and told me to follow him. It was strange; as I walked, my body felt so light I thought I could fly. He seemed to be reading my thoughts because every time I thought something, he answered.

"We came to a short flight of stairs and walked into a room, which was full of people. We walked by the entrance to another room and I could see five beautiful women sitting there, smiling. They were dressed in glowing gowns of the most vivid red, blue, and green that I have ever seen. I wanted to go into the room and talk to them, but Auriel looked at me and said, 'You can't talk to them yet. Since they are on a higher level and your quantum vibration signature is not matched to theirs, it would cause problems.'

"He led me to a room where he introduced me to a man that looked like his brother. Auriel said, 'This is Aerial and he is a doctor. He is going to help you with your work.' The 'doctor' took me by the arm into a room as Auriel said good-bye. The doctor then asked me to lie on a table. The room was bare except for the table, which was the color of gold and was glowing with a red light. I lay on the table and the doctor waived his right arm, and a device that looked like a gold DVD appeared and hovered above my forehead. Then the disk began to vibrate and I could feel energy of some sort going into my head. Then the doctor opened up his hands, and there were three ruby-like crystals. He placed them one by one on my head, and I could feel them being sucked into my brain. He said, 'We are finished. You can go home.' I got up and heard a buzzing in my head and, before I could say anything, the doctor said, 'Not to worry, the sound will go away before you are back in your world.'

"Then a man came to the entrance of the doctor's room. He was human and had dark hair. He put his hand on my shoulder and told me to follow him. As I did, he said, 'We are going to take you back to your car and on the road.' I asked him if he was from another planet. He said that he was from Earth and that he was taken three hundred years ago to work with this group of angels. We went back to the hangar and my car was there. I got in and then there was a flash of light, and I was back on the road again, driving home.

"The next morning I got up and started writing; in about ten hours I had a manuscript that was five hundred pages long. The strange thing is, I can't remember writing the material nor did I feel the passage of time. I thought I was only writing for a half-hour and did one page. I was shocked to see what I had done, but it was in my handwriting and about three-quarters through it I changed pens and I don't recall doing this. I had to read what I wrote because I had no idea what was on the paper. Since that time I have produced two more manuscripts that I hope will some day be published."

Henry's ability to produce manuscripts in a very short time is similar to that of Dean Fagerstrom, whose case is presented in *Contact of the 5th Kind*. Like Henry, Dean has produced two complete three-hundred-page manuscripts, which were channeled by one of these "angelic" beings. As of 2006, Henry claims that he has not visually seen this Auriel since the last encounter, but has heard his voice a number of times. Henry says that Auriel is still working through him, producing written text material about God, spiritual development, and the state of the seen and unseen universe so that one day they can be used as teaching materials in the new world of humanity. I have read both manuscripts and they are very well written and filled with deep spiritual teachings that in my opinion could not have come from Henry's limited educational background. Henry Miller and Dean Fagerstrom are two individuals who, in my mind, without a doubt, are in contact with an intelligence that is not of this Earth.

EIGHT

THE TRICK
OF THE MAGICIAN

We humans are very limited when it comes to perceiving things outside our five senses. We need instruments to discover and study types of energy and phenomena that lie outside the abilities of these senses. If we cannot observe and study a phenomenon with our senses or the instruments available to us with current technology, many will say that it just can't exist. UFOs are outside our normal realm of reality, and trying to understand them with conventional means is like a child sitting in the audience watching a master magician performing an act on stage. The magician does all these amazing things that appear to be magic, but the child was told by his parents and teachers that there is so such thing as magic. However, the child continues to watch the magician and can't figure out how things can disappear, reappear, and change shape right in front of his eyes.

The child then leans over and whispers in his father's ear and says, "Dad, how is the magician doing this?" The father replies, "I don't know." Now this really confuses the child since his parents told him that magic does not exist. The child now thinks, *If magic does not exist, then how can these tricks be performed in front of hundreds of adults and no one can explain how it's done?* The child then comes to a conclusion and says, "If my parents can't tell me how it's all done, then it must be magic." From the child's point of view it is magic, but we know the magician is apparently doing magical things because of a clever trick. The child sits there, watching and studying every move of the magician, trying to figure out how the trick was done, but he cannot. Unless the magician takes the child on the stage and shows him how the "trick" is done, the child will never figure it out.

The UFO experience is like this—we are the child in the audience and the intelligences behind the UFO phenomenon, whether they are extraterrestrials, jinn, or angels, are the magician, and this magician keeps his tricks secret and will not share them with humanity. We will never be able to solve the UFO mystery by methods of conventional research since the intelligence behind it, especially the jinn, can manipulate evidence to lead UFO researchers in the wrong direction and send them running in circles like dogs chasing their own tails.

THEN WHY BOTHER WITH THE RESEARCH?

We are trying to use the science, logic, and technology of a material universe to track down and study beings that are not physical in form and can manipulate matter and change their own shape. Over the past decade, science has gained a great understanding of the "seen" universe, but we still are blind to the unseen universe and despite our advances, we are still being led around blindly by intelligences like the jinn. The jinn can appear like extraterrestrials and even create the illusion of flying saucers. Some of the jinn appear like the Virgin Mary, while others can appear like monsters, demons, fallen angels, or reptilian or insect-like creatures. Some jinn make direct contact with humans, while others use the game of channeling. Since creatures like the jinn leave no physical trace of their existence, people who have made contact with them have no physical evidence to show. Once we know about the jinn and how they play their games with humans and most likely other physical beings in the universe, then we can continue to do UFO and paranormal research and gain a better understanding of creation without being taken in by the cosmos's greatest tricksters.

THE BEING OF SMOKE

The following encounter with a jinn-like entity took place on December 20, 2003, in Litchfield, Connecticut. The witness is a fifty-year-old male who has a background in electrical engineering. In this case study, we shall call him Mike, since that is his real first name, but his last name is not given in order to protect his identity. The following is his story as told to me shortly after his experience.

"It was nighttime in the winter and the moon was out very bright in the clear sky. I live alone and my street is a dead end, and there is quite a bit of space between houses. I like this area because I prefer my privacy, but that night I wished I had a great number of neighbors so that I could call them to come and see this thing. I went outside to get some air and clear my head because I was working on this project for IBM, which was designing a power relay station for one of their main computer rooms, and it was starting to get to me because I couldn't figure out how the wiring should go through the junctions without burning the building down.

"I went outside and looked up and saw a dark cigar-like object up in the sky, hanging there like a giant blimp with no lights. At first that's what I thought it was, a blimp. It was right above my yard and not that high. I said to myself, 'What the hell is this guy doing just hanging in the sky with no lights?' Then all of a sudden there was a flash of pink light and in my yard was this figure that looked like a man made of smoke. I have about an acre in my front yard, so he was pretty far away, but I could make him out. He looked like he was made of gray smoke, and his form was being illuminated by the moon. At that point I don't know what happened to the object in the sky, since my eyes were transfixed on this man or whatever it was slowly walking towards my front door. I then heard the dogs in the neighborhood start howling and barking and this figure kept on walking towards me. I called out, 'Can I help you, whoever you are?' I even said, 'Who goes there?' This thing was now less than one hundred feet away from me and still getting closer. It looked just like a man made of smoke. It was about seven feet tall and very slim, and I could see no face or hands, just arms, head, legs, and a body.

"I quickly went back into the house and closed the door and pulled down the shades, then the lights went out and that really freaked me out. I went to the phone to call the police, but the phone was dead. Then all of a sudden there was pounding on the door and the walls of my home. The pounding was so loud and strong that things were flying off a shelf I had in the living room. I ran upstairs and got a baseball bat to protect myself. As I was walking back down the stairs, I heard what sounded like voices in the living room. I could not understand what they were saying; it sounded like a chant or prayer in some strange language.

"I went downstairs and yelled, 'Okay, you want a piece of me? Then come and get it!' and I started swinging the bat as I was walking down the stairs and into the living room, knocking lamps and breaking my television in the process. Then all of a sudden the voices stopped and the lights went back on. Still shaking, I grabbed for the phone and thanked God it was working and called the police. Two officers came over in about ten minutes and took a report. I could tell that the officers did not believe me, and they asked me if I was drinking or did drugs. I have never seen a ghost or had anything happen to me that was supernatural or whatever, but this changed my mind and made me realize that we are not the only living beings sharing this planet."

Mike's experience and encounter with the smoke-like being would have puzzled the hell out of a UFO investigator looking for aliens and spaceships. However, once we consider that there are multiple dimensions, other parallel realities, we can understand and make more sense out of his encounter.

FALLING STONES FROM NOWHERE

After re-analyzing the many unexplained cases in my files, I discovered that just before UFOs appear there is an outbreak of paranormal events. People who are not psychic become so, and those who are psychic report an increase in their ability. It must take a great deal of energy to open these dimensional windows, and perhaps a burst of energy is released, which could power spontaneous psychic phenomena.

One of the more common paranormal events that occurs before a UFO "flap" (a great number of sightings and encounters in a small area, for example the Hudson Valley sightings) is the falling of rocks from the sky or the moving and teleportation of stones from the ground to the air. Rocks falling from the sky apparently out of thin air have been reported since the early days of the Roman Empire and although it is not an everyday event, there have been enough cases over the centuries to document the phenomenon. Before I present a case study of a rock-falling event that I personally investigated in Connecticut, let me give you a brief history of the flying rocks, which many researchers consider a form of poltergeist activity.

POLTERGEIST OR METEORITES?

The great scientists of eighteenth-century Europe often investigated claims of stones falling from the sky but were very skeptical of the occurrence. When a number of stones were brought to them over the years by farmers who claimed they fell from the sky, the scientists looked at them, touched them, and examined them with the limited scientific technology that they had at that time and just shook their heads. The top scientific minds during the eighteenth century like Lavoisier, Gassendi, and Herschel could not accept the idea that stones could fall from the sky, so they labeled these claims as foolish, hoaxes, or the product of an overactive imagination.

At about the same time in the United States, Native American medicine men from the Algonquian, Hopi, and Pawnee tribes claimed that in their medicine pouches they had "star stones"—actual stones that fell from the stars, which they used for healing since they contained "powerful magic." Once again the scientists at the time considered it primitive superstition, because it was impossible for a stone to fall from the sky. Well, it turns out that the stones recovered by the farmers in Europe and the star stones of the medicine men were actually meteorites and they did fall from the sky.

The scientists and the learned people at the time told everyone that it was nonsense to believe that a rock can fall from the sky, but today we know that is possible and the keepers and professors of knowledge at that time were wrong. There is an old saying that states, "Being a genius and very well educated does not guarantee that you will be correct in all of your assumptions; you just might be dead wrong." If you take a close look at this story, it sounds a great deal like what is taking place today in the academic world concerning their attitude about UFOs and paranormal phenomena. The professors of knowledge of today are saying that these things can't be happening, that it is impossible, and that the stories of aliens, UFO sightings, and poltergeists must be the result of the overactive imagination of a bored society, unstable people, or just simply a hoax to get publicity and to make money.

It's one thing when a single rock falls from the sky and something totally different when it rains stones of all sizes on an entire neighborhood in front of many witnesses.

THE SKY IS FALLING

That's what people must have thought long ago when rocks would fall from a clear blue sky, apparently materializing out of thin air. The *New York Times* on May 1, 1821, reported that a shower of stones fell upon a house in Durham, North Carolina, for at least ten minutes at a time. This happened several times during the month of April, and despite placing guards and soldiers around the house, the mayor of the town could not find the cause. On more than one occasion, several of the police officers investigating the event saw the stones apparently materializing about thirty feet above the house and falling straight down. During the end of each event, there were at least fifty stones that fell out of thin air, ranging in size from two to five inches across.

On September 5, 1866, in Charleston, South Carolina, stones fell from the sky and bounced off the pavement on the streets and sidewalk. The few witnesses who did see this event take place reported that it happened at about three in the morning and that the stones were warm to the touch. The strange thing about this case is that although there were hundreds of stones, they were confined to an area with a diameter of less than fifty feet.

In May of 1922, the owner of a pharmacy shop in Hartford, Connecticut, reported that for several months at three in the morning, his shop and apartment upstairs was bombarded by stones that fell from the sky. Police were sent to investigate and thought someone was using a slingshot device from a nearby hill or building as a joke. The next morning at 3:00 a.m., police staked out the area and, with surprise, witnessed stones ranging in size from a pebble to five or so inches in diameter beginning to fall on the shop, apparently from the sky. The police found no human cause and when one of the officers picked up a stone, he reported that it was warm, almost hot, to the touch. The rock falling continued intermediately for several months, and each time when the police were present all they could do was just stand in awe as the rocks rained from the sky and only fell upon the shop.

There are many more reports of rock-falling incidents from all over the world throughout recorded history. However, let's focus on one case that took place in the twentieth century that I personally investigated in my home state of Connecticut.

THE EICHLER'S COVE POLTERGEIST

Many psychic researchers claim that the falling of stones is centered on one person, usually a young girl or boy in their teens; such may have been the case in 1978, when stones fell from the sky in a small neighborhood in central Connecticut. I personally investigated this case and could find no natural cause for the paranormal event. It is important to mention that several days after the rock falling stopped, UFOs appeared in the area, as well as reports of animal mutilations.

The force that was responsible for the rock-falling event that has mystified police and residents of the area may never be known for sure, but there is no doubt in the minds of the people who live there that it did take place, and there was no conventional explanation. Eichler's Cove is a small community near Monroe, Connecticut, and it has never been known as a center for paranormal events. The people go about their everyday business not thinking about UFOs, ghosts, or poltergeists. The rocks began to fall on homes in the community on August 11, 1978, and continued almost every night until August 31. Police were baffled and could not find the cause, and they speculated that a "bunch of kids" were using a catapult on the nearby hill to shoot rocks at the homes. The rocks ranged in size from small pebbles to boulders fourteen pounds or more, and since the hill was a quarter of a mile away, police investigators were baffled about how the perpetrators could shoot the rocks from a homemade catapult with such great accuracy.

During the August 17 incident, the rocks began falling at 8:00 p.m. sharp and rained down on top of three homes and a gazebo, all within a one-hundred-fifty-foot radius. Police investigators were present at the time and saw the rocks appear out of thin air and fall straight down. At the same time this was taking place, police officers went over to the hill and searched the entire area but found no human cause for the rock fall. The local chief of police still could not accept the fact that there was no explanation for the event and was quoted as saying, "I have been a police officer for forty years, and in that time I never had to deal with ghosts and I do not plan to now" (quote taken from a police statement made by the chief to a reporter from the local newspaper, the *Newtown Bee*, August 25, 1978).

On a number of occasions, some neighbors who live in the area were struck by the rocks, but except for some minor bruises they were not seriously injured. During an evening rock fall, Newtown police officer Detective Harry Noroian was hit in the head by a flying stone, causing a cut in his head. Witnesses then reported that the same stone that struck the officer levitated off the ground and jumped like a rock skipping across water, landing over ten feet away. On August 21, residents who lived in the area reported seeing dozens of rocks flying straight into the air from behind a stand of trees then coming straight down on the homes, causing the people who were outside to seek shelter. Police investigation later determined that even a strong man could not hurl the larger stones from a location that distant and achieve that much height above the homes. They also ruled out the catapult theory, since it would be impossible to have all the rocks land in the same location with that much accuracy. Eichler's Cove then became the subject of speculation in the supernatural realm, and when the story hit the local and national press, news reporters from radio and television showed up in the hope of capturing the mischievous "ghost" on film.

The paranormal event was investigated by a member of the Psychical Research Foundation (PRF) and me. We both came to the conclusion that kids throwing rocks were not responsible for this event, as was still speculated by police. The

PRF researcher came to the conclusion that the rock-falling episode was the result of some type of psychic kinesis done unconsciously by a young girl or boy while asleep. Although the police did not accept this theory, I considered it and used it as a foundation to continue my own investigation.

TRACKING DOWN THE
EICHLER'S COVE POLTERGEIST

When I arrived at the scene, most of the activity had stopped. I began interviewing each of the witnesses and soon realized that there was no connection between them that could have caused the phenomenon to take place. None of the people I interviewed had any psychic ability, and until that time they had never had any type of paranormal experience. The poltergeist activity seemed to be centered around one particular home, and while interviewing the adult residents, their twelve-year-old son came into the living room and said, "I never saw the rocks falling, but I dreamt about them." I asked him what he meant. He replied, "Before it happened, I dreamt about it and many times when I go to sleep, I dream about the rocks falling from the sky and find out when I wake up that it really happened." His parents told me that he had some problems that were emotional and the doctor they were seeing (psychiatrist) gave him medicine that would relieve his anxiety and allow him to sleep. I asked the parents what times he received the medication and tried to correlate his nap time with the falling stones. In every case, it was apparent that the stones started falling while this child was asleep.

I had heard that poltergeist activity can sometimes be traced to a teen or preteen who is having emotional problems, and phenomena like the psychokinetic movement of material objects have been reported taking place while they are in a deep sleep. The next evening at about eight thirty, I visited this home and the boy was asleep. As I was talking to the parents, a police car pulled up. I looked out the window and saw an officer looking around. As I was going out to greet the officer, I heard loud thumps on the roof and ran outside to see two stones fall from the sky. The officer was standing there in amazement and said, "They just dropped from the sky." As soon as he finished that statement, one of the rocks that was on the ground, weighing about two pounds, jumped into the air and struck the officer on the arm, bruising him. I picked up the rock and it was warm to the touch. I put the rock in my bag and today it still remains in my collection. I asked for a ladder and climbed up to the roof to find it covered with rocks with an average size of about three inches across scattered all along the roof and in the gutters. Although some of the other homes close by also had rocks on them, the home of the boy had at least four times as many.

The boy was finally admitted to a mental hospital and after that, the rock falls ceased. Later I discovered that this "mentally ill" young man reported seeing "aliens" in the area and claimed to have conversations with a being that he called Iblsas. (Could it be Iblis?) This entity told the boy that he was from another dimension that was close by and chose him to help rescue his people so that they can come into the physical world. Instead of finding out if the experience was real, the doctors immediately labeled him as psychotic and pumped the drug Thorazine into his bloodstream twice a day. It could very well be that the boy had psychic abilities, and when the portal to this other dimension opened and contact with the being Iblsas began, the boy absorbed the energy and, in his sleep, subconsciously generated psychokinetic phenomena in the form of rock teleportation. A well-known paranormal writer and researcher once told me that most likely our mental institutions are filled with psychics and people who claim ET contact. We may be locking away people who were chosen by an interdimensional intelligence to be ambassadors for a new age.

THE FIGURE EIGHT IN THE SKY

Soon after the rock-falling incident, UFOs appeared during the night over the Connecticut towns of Monroe, Newtown, Sandy Hook, and Danbury. On September 3, I received a call from Newtown police giving me the names of people who had had a sighting in the last two hours. That evening I talked to four individuals whose sightings were just about identical, that is, a bright object in the sky that was the shape of a yellow egg. The object would hover and then move so fast in a pattern that looked like an illuminated figure eight or infinity sign in the sky. The object then would once again become stationary and emit bright sparks that seemed to reach the ground in the distance. The object appeared three more times during September 3, 15, and 21. During its last appearance on September 21, as residents of Newtown were watching it flicker in the sky, it just went out like a "light be-ing turned off" and vanished. During the object's appearance on all three dates, there were confirmed power outages in the towns of Sandy Hook and Newtown. The power com-pany could find no cause for the power loss, and it still re-mains a mystery today. During that time, there was one close encounter reported to me by a resident of Newtown, Con-necticut. The following is his story, from October of 1978.

THE UFO AND THE BRIDGE

"I was driving home alone on September 1 at about 8:30 p.m. after a hard day's work. I crossed the bridge near Clearwater road, which is short and made of metal. It was a clear late summer night and I was alone, anxious to get back to my family in Newtown. As I started to cross the bridge, the ra-dio started getting a great deal of static. Then all of a sudden the car died, but the headlights were still on. I said to myself, 'Oh shit, what a place to break down.' I grabbed a flashlight in the glove compartment and popped the hood to take a look. As I walked out of the car, my attention was drawn to this bright light just above the bridge. It was flickering colors like yellow, green, and red, and at first I thought it was the planet Jupiter, which I'd heard was bright in the sky second only to Venus. I looked under the hood and couldn't see any-thing wrong. I looked up and saw the light getting lower and lower. Now I could see that it wasn't a planet but a disk-like object. It got so bright that I had to shield my eyes.

"I ran back into the car, and the light from the object was so bright that the metal on the bridge was being illuminated by it. Then sparks like flares shot from it in all directions and two red, glowing balls came down from the UFO and circled over and under the bridge. Then they came up and circled around my car, moving slow enough that I could make out their shape. They were about the size of a baseball and they had this steady red color, almost like crimson. Then the two lights went up into the object and the thing just disappeared. Then I was sitting in the dark, and I looked up and the entire bridge was glowing like it just got charged up. It was a faint blue-white glow and it was brightest on the support beams of the bridge. Then, after about thirty seconds, the glow faded and my radio came back on, and I was able to start up my car. I drove home and found out from the television that there were UFO sightings in the area. I told my wife what I saw; she believed me but told me not to tell the children, who were six and nine years old, since they might get scared and not want to go to bed."

ANIMAL MUTILATIONS WERE NEXT

Animal mutilations, especially involving cattle, have been taking place in North America for over one hundred years. Since 1960, the number of cattle and other animals that are found mysteriously mutilated have increased. I don't profess to know what is causing the mutilations or why, but they are a reality and seem somehow to be connected with UFO sightings.

Several years ago, while promoting my book *Night Siege: The Hudson Valley UFO Sightings*, I was a guest on a radio show in New York City. At that time, there were recent cattle mutilations taking place in Alabama. The host of the radio show called the sheriff's department of the county where the dead cattle were found and had a "head sheriff" on the phone as part of the show. The officer said he was called by cattlemen because they found their cows dead in the pasture. When he arrived at the scene, he examined the animals and they had surgical cuts in them, and things like sexual organs, eyes, and ears removed. He said that they were also drained of blood, and insects, scavengers, and predators would not touch the carcasses.

As I listened to him, it became apparent that despite his twenty-plus years in law enforcement, he was quite freaked out by the entire thing. He also mentioned that on numerous occasions, strange groups of lights were seen over the fields, and the next day several cattle would be found dead in that area. The sheriff ruled out things like predators and a human cause, since there were no tracks in the ground. The sheriff then began to tell a chilling story of a farmer and his prize cow that was pregnant. At dusk, the farmer checked on the cow and planned to return it to the barn, but went back to his home first to make an important telephone call. The person he was calling was not in, so he went back to the field to put the cow in the barn. When he arrived at the field, he was shocked to see the cow lying dead with sharp cuts in its body. What really frightened him was that the fetus was also taken out of the womb and mutilated the same way as the mother. He could not have been gone more than five minutes, yet, amazing as it sounds, the mutilation took place within that time. He called police and they found no tracks or evidence of a struggle, and the farmer reported that he heard nothing.

According to the sheriff, the only thing unusual that was found was a powdery residue of magnesium oxide and potassium oxide on the cow's back. I found this interesting, since in several of the cases of UFO landings that I had investigated, I also found a residue on the ground in a circular shape. This residue also turned out to be magnesium oxide and potassium oxide. Was this the connection between the mutilations and the UFOs?

ANIMAL MUTILATIONS IN CONNECTICUT

Shortly after the UFO sightings in the Newtown/Monroe area of Connecticut, right around late September and early October of 1978, a local sheep owner went out to his pasture and was shocked to find his sheep dead. All twenty-two of his prize-winning sheep were scattered over ten acres of land, and the strange thing about it was that he was just there the night before to check on them and they were fine. He called animal control at the Newtown police station, and at once an officer was sent to investigate. He was told it was most likely a pack of wild dogs that killed his sheep. The owner disagreed since when sheep are attacked by a predator, they bunch up together for protection. These sheep were found scattered over a large area as if something wanted to isolate each animal. Furthermore, dogs bring down four-legged animals from the legs, and there were no bite marks on the extremities of the sheep. One week later, eleven more sheep were found dead within one mile of the first location and killed the same way. In both cases, the investigators could not find any tracks and the fence that enclosed the property was not damaged at all.

I went out to take a look at the sheep, and they had large slits in their throats where it appears their blood was drained. The soft parts of their stomachs were missing, not torn out, but the wounds were smooth as if done by a very sharp knife, or perhaps a laser. Although the weather was still warm, insects and other scavengers like birds stayed away from the dead animals.

In the weeks to follow, rabbits, ducks, geese, swans, dogs, and cats were also found dead and mutilated in the area. The local sheepherders were told that stray dogs were to blame, and they began to fire at family dogs that got loose from their owners and strayed onto or near their property. On one occasion, a family's English setter was shot by a sheep rancher because the dog came close to his property border. According to the family, the dog was gentle and would not have hurt the sheep, but the owner of the sheep said he wasn't taking any chances. Then, as quickly as they started, the animal deaths stopped and, to my knowledge, never took place again.

SKY CRITTERS AND SPOOK LIGHT

Cattle, horse, and other animal mutilations are a mystery. How can they be done so quickly and without a sound from the animal? Who is to blame for this perplexing carnage? Is it the aliens who are using the cattle for experiments and feeding? Is it a paramilitary organization or the government conducting secret genetic experiments and harvesting a new killer virus in the blood cells of cows? Or is it something else that is causing these deaths across the world, something very elusive, like a creature of our nightmares?

About forty years ago, a paranormal researcher by the name of Trevor James Constable found out that when infrared film is used in a camera with a very fast shutter speed in a location that is at high altitude and very dry, the film picks up images that look like flying saucers. He also noticed that some of the images also looked like a stingrays or jellyfish. Constable speculated that in our atmosphere is a life form that is invisible to us because it moves very fast and radiates a great deal of infrared radiation from its body.

Since infrared radiation cannot be seen by the human eye, the creature would be almost invisible. Constable then called these creatures sky critters, and today the notion that they might exist is all but forgotten in circles of UFO research, especially within groups like CUFOS or MUFON that are looking for nuts-and-bolts spaceships, which they feel can explain all sightings. As Constable says in his book *The Cosmic Pulse of Life*, "The existence of these organisms seems to be plasmatic, having the outline of their form expressed in heat substance. They travel in a pulsating fashion, swelling and shrinking cyclically as they move through the air."

So what about these sky critters? Can we list them as a possibility, being one small part of the UFO puzzle? You bet we can! When the dimensional windows open, there is a rush of energy into our world and not only do the interdimensional beings come through, but also other living creatures that exist in that dimension may be pulled in unintentionally and trapped in our universe, where they appear to us like totally alien life forms.

Sky critters may be the cause of the animal mutilations, and they could be feeding on them. Since these "critters" move so fast and are invisible to the human eye, a group of them might be able to swoop down from the sky and feed on a number of cows or sheep in a matter of seconds. The late, great paranormal researcher Ivan T. Sanderson had this to say concerning the sky critters in his book *Uninvited Visitors*: "They are Unidentified Aerial Objects, but they don't look like machines at all. They look to a biologist [Ivan was a biologist] like horribly unicellular life forms, complete in some cases with nuclei, vacuoles and other organelles. Some are even amoebic in form." I have seen Constable's photographs and they do make a strong case for the existence of these creatures, and although I have never photographed or seen one when investigating a UFO sighting, I consider them to be part of the complex UFO puzzle. If you have a 35mm camera, and then get a roll of infrared film and a Wratten 25A red filter and go to a high place at sunrise or sunset and take a few pictures of the sky, you might catch one of these critters swooping about in the atmosphere looking for a way to go home.

SPOOK LIGHT

Spook or ghost lights are a phenomenon that is well documented—there are cases all over the world of mysterious balls of light that seem to follow people and then move away when you try to approach them. The phantom lights behave more like playful animals rather than a highly intelligent being. Spook light has been imaged using film and digital cameras in and around the stone chambers of New York State. Once again I believe that these stone chambers were built by Druid and Celtic explorers thousands of years ago and that they mark the location of a portal or window. This could be the reason why this "spook light" is imaged and observed in and around these chambers. It could be that one or more of these poor lost creatures are hanging around the door waiting for it to open so that they can go home.

I personally do believe that other creatures from this parallel reality do mistakenly make their way into our dimension. I have witnessed spook light in action and can tell you that it acts more like a thinking life form than some electrical phenomenon of nature like piezoelectric sparks.

NINE

A UNIVERSE
OF POSSIBILITIES

Our view of the universe has changed considerably since I was a child growing up in the fifties. My interest in science was sparked by the many science fiction movies that I saw on television. During those early days, our view of the cosmos was three-dimensional, and most scientists were still perplexed by Einstein's special theory of relativity. Today it's quite a different story—with new ideas like string and superstring theory, we find the physical universe could have as many as twenty-one dimensions! This multidimensional universe is not only in the deepest reaches of space, but it is also all around us right here on planet Earth. A multidimensional universe can explain why a great deal of phenomena like UFOs and poltergeists has escaped our understanding all of these years.

When we look out into space, it appears flat and two-dimensional, but astronomers do get a hint that it is indeed multidimensional, since there are galaxies located below us, above us, and to the sides. However, we are three-dimensional beings and are restricted in our view of the cosmos and cannot perceive a multidimensional universe since we are limited to seeing only three ways—up, down, and sideways. We can use an ordinary garden hose as an example to better understand these limitations.

THE GARDEN HOSE AND THE UNIVERSE

When we look at a garden hose from a distance, it looks quite flat, and from that point of view it only appears to have one dimension—its width. As we get closer to the garden hose, we see that it not only has width, but it curves on each side and a whole new dimension has been added. As we get closer and examine the hose and pick it up, we see that it not only has width but length and a circumference. Then comes the big surprise: it is also hollow and has an extra dimension inside, an entirely new area of existence that was totally unknown to us until we picked it up and looked inside.

With the technology that we now have, our view of the universe is limited to observing only three dimensions, much like the person studying the garden hose from a distance. So where are all these dimensions and why can't we see them? Current theory states that the fourth spatial dimension is located at a right angle to a right angle. This is a direction in physical space where you just can't turn fast enough to see, since as you turn you are in fact locked into the fabric of space itself. It's like being under a blanket and trying to turn in circles to look above the fabric covering your head—as you turn, it turns with you. I am sure there are beings in the universe with a very advanced technology that do use four dimensions for traveling across the fabric of space and then perhaps they also can readjust their point in time. To us humans on Earth, it is still a theory with a great number of questions that need to be answered.

FLATLAND

In reality, we are very limited three-dimensional beings who cannot see into the fourth dimension of space and time, but just what is the fourth dimension? Perhaps you have heard of it before or watched futuristic space explorers in the movies or on a sci-fi television show as they navigate through distant sections of the physical universe and travel back and forth in time. Actually, no one really knows what four-dimensional space is like because we just haven't been there. We are told by the theorist that it is a dimension located in the physical universe, a parallel reality, a place all around us that can exist in all points of time.

To most people this might sound confusing, so let me give you an example by comparing it with a hypothetical two-dimensional being trying to perceive our three-dimensional existence. The idea, which is still used today, originally came from an 1884 novel by Edwin Abbott entitled, *Flatland: A Romance of Many Dimensions*. In this short book, the author uses the idea of a being who lives in a two-dimensional world called "Flatland" and is trying to explain to his peers the existence of a three-dimensional world. The idea for the story was considerably ahead of its time and although it is not very scientific in nature, it was used to point out the political and social ignorance in Mr. Abbott's day.

Imagine there is a two-dimensional world called Flatland. Here in Flatland are a great number of two-dimensional beings. They are completely flat, and they have width and length, but no height. A good example of what a being like this may be like is a shadow. A shadow can exist right in the same space as a physical object and go practically undetected. Since a two-dimensional life form has no height, the thickness of a sheet of paper, when placed in front of this being, would extend higher than it could see.

So let's say that there are these hypothetical people in Flatland and although we have a detailed view of their world, they can only get a minuscule glimpse of ours. The ones who do get this dimensional glimpse of our reality may try to report it to the Flatland authorities, who may in turn try to explain it as natural phenomena, swamp gas, or perhaps the overactive imagination of a disturbed Flatland citizen. If you place the tip of your finger in Flatland, they would only see the very base of your finger; they could not see what lies above. As you move your finger around, the strange object that appeared before them will seem to change shape. When you lift up your finger, from their point of view it will mysteriously disappear.

Now you go to another area of Flatland and see a group of these two-dimensional beings talking and you decide you want to make contact with one, so you reach down and pick it up and bring him into three-dimensional space. From the point of view of his fellow Flatlanders, their friend simply vanished into thin air; however, their friend is now in a new part of the universe. He can still hear his friends talking and tries to call out, but perhaps he is not heard or they hear him very faintly but can't tell where the voice is coming from.

You now have this flat person in your hand and you move him up and down, but remember he is still two-dimensional and can only see a thin line, so he does not get a real view of this strange new world, just a narrow glimpse of it. Finally you realize this communication is not going to work, so you place him back among his friends who see him just reappear out of thin air. They ask him, "Where did you go?" The confused Flatlander tries to point in the direction he went to, but since he can only see and move backwards, forwards, and sideways, he can't show his friends where this place was that he was taken to. He also tries to explain what he saw, but cannot describe it, since no Flatlander has ever experienced this before and they have no language to describe all the new things in the strange world. Finally, he tries to tell this amazing story of his experience, but most do not believe him. His experience into this new world is finally published in a tabloid called the *Flatland Enquirer*. His friends and superiors read the story and suggest that he should seek professional help. Sound familiar?

THE MULTIDIMENSIONAL UNIVERSE

This is the problem that we three-dimensional humans face when shown pieces of the fourth dimension. Like the Flatlander, we can only perceive a part of this other dimension and try to interpret what little of it we saw with a language that cannot describe new objects, beings, colors, or dimensions.

In reality, all parts of the multidimensional universe can exist together in the same space, and like multiple beams of light traveling through air or water, there is very little interaction between them. Alternate dimensions can exist in the same physical area, but at different frequencies to each other and at different angles. A simple example of this is a number of plastic cups that can fit into one another. They all occupy the same general space, but at different levels—our universe may have a similar geometry. Our physical universe may have as many as twenty-one dimensions with ten of them tightly wound in physical space. The cosmos may be even more complex than we imagine, with not only a physical universe, but also one of plasma and energy, each possessing a multitude of dimensions.

The energy that we are familiar with in our physical reality is electromagnetic and photonic in nature, and it is formed when atoms vibrate. Our physical universe may be the result of another dimension of energy that flows into it, a real existence of which our reality is merely an expression. For decades astronomers thought that the cosmos was expanding and slowing down, running out of the energy from the Big Bang, a giant explosion that created the physical universe. Recently, astronomers were shocked to find out that the universe is not slowing down, but speeding up. This force that is speeding up the universe and pushing the galaxies farther apart has been called the "Dark Force" or "Dark Energy," by scientists, since it cannot be seen or detected by our instruments. We do see the result of this Dark Energy, since the galaxies are moving farther and farther from each other and the greater the distance a galaxy is from our home galaxy, the Milky Way, the faster it seems to be receding from us. Could this Dark Energy be coming into our reality from another dimension, providing the power to run our universe?

STRING THEORY AND THE
MULTIDIMENSIONAL UNIVERSE

String theory is a new idea that states that particles that exist in the universe do not lie at zero dimension points, but are on building blocks or lines called strings. This theory unifies the forces of nature into a single one and tells that all of creation is linked together. The "vibration" of a string at a particular frequency determines if that particle that makes up the cosmos is to be an electron, photon, or any other bit of matter. The force that causes the string to vibrate may come from another universe. In order for one string not to interfere with another when it is vibrating, something like a membrane may separate them. A string can be opened or closed; open strings are linear while closed strings can fold space, creating a multitude of dimensions.

In the 1990s, Edward Witten found evidence that string theory can predict the existence of an eleven-dimensional universe—this is called the M theory. Many recent developments in the field led to the idea that the universe could have has many as twenty-six dimensions. The hope that scientists have is that string theory will be able to unify all the known forces and particles into a single theory of "all and everything."

SUPERSTRINGS

Strings interact by splitting and joining. The annihilation of two closed strings into a single closed string creates changes to the dimensional state of space. Multiple closed strings can be connected to make tunnels that can transport you to another part of the universe or even to another dimension. This is one way in which dimensional wormholes or Dr. Hynek's windows can be formed. Look at it this way: If you have two lengths of string crossing over each other, each string would represent a part of the physical universe. If we bend the strings to form a loop, we can merge both dimensions together, and twisting each string can bring us to different levels or, in the case of the cosmos, different dimensions. Each part of the string could actually vibrate at a different rate, which would mean "time" as we know it will progress in a different manner depending upon where you are located on the string.

VIEWING THESE OTHER DIMENSIONS

How can one see into these other dimensions? I really don't know the answer to this question. Being trapped in a physical body that has three dimensions makes it impossible to move into higher realms without some type of assistance. I heard a rumor some years ago that a research team at Princeton University was experimenting with high-frequency generators and was able to actually bend three-dimensional space, allowing them to get a quick glimpse of a four-dimensional universe. When the generator was turned on maximum, strange spheres of lights appeared in the room, displaying colors that are unknown to the visible light spectrum. The researchers also reported that images of different points in time appeared, and finally a giant insect-like being came into view as the generator caught on fire. When they tried to repeat the experiment, nothing happened and when human beings were placed in the center of the field they became disoriented and remained in a confused state for several hours.

Images of phantom people, armies, and ships have been reported for centuries. Since the age of photography, images have appeared on film that were not in the scenery. For example, one case that I worked on years ago involved one of the best examples of paranormal photography that I have ever seen. Two young girls (who also had previous UFO contact experiences) were photographing flowers on Block Island, which is off the East Coast of the United States. As the images on a 36-exposure roll of color slide film began at frame 1, the photographers' reality (shooting flowers on the island) was replaced by images of places and people that did not seem to be part of our time. By frame 20, there was only one reality on the film and it wasn't the flowers on Block Island. The images included bridges, people dressed in clothes that seemed to be from around the mid-to-late nineteenth century, and a wall showing pictographs of a bull, a man with wings (Nephilim?), and what appeared to be a bust of a minotaur. A detailed investigation was carried out on the prints and negatives, and they were not found to be double exposures or any type of developing flaw.

It may be possible that the way to enter the fourth dimension is to curve space at a right angle to a right angle, allowing the fabric of space or strings to overlap. The fourth dimension may be a place where all points of time merge and every possible event of reality branches off from one dimension to the next and perhaps in another point in time. The fourth dimension may be the dimensional hub to the multidimensional universe.

SO WHAT IS TIME?

Time is not a physical thing; it is something that exists in the minds of human beings. In short, time as a force simply does not exist. It has been proven that as you approach the speed of light or in the influence of a strong gravitational field, time slows down. Time is measured by the movement of our planet's revolution and rotation (a year and solar day, respectively). Our clocks are set to solar time, or the time it takes for the sun to rise and then rise once again. As three-dimensional beings, we are caught in the motion of the linear movement of the expanding universe. From one second to the next, you are not in the same place in the cosmos, since the sun and the planets are orbiting the galaxy and our galaxy is moving out into space and speeding up. Therefore, from one nanosecond to the next, the atoms that make up your body are increasing in vibration at the quantum level, causing you to change frequency. In short, from one nanosecond to the next, you have actually shifted in frequency, causing you to move into another point in time. If we were to exist in the fourth dimension, then we could be at any point in time and space, since we would no longer be bound by the laws of the linear expansion of the universe. A four-dimensional being who was never exposed to laws of a three-dimensional universe might not understand the concept of what we call time, because past, present, and future exist together in its dimension. If our idea of a multidimensional universe is correct, then it would be possible to travel forward and backward in time.

Each year, conventional scientists discover more about the state of the universe, yet many of these new discoveries were in fact proposed centuries ago by philosophers and mystics such as Gregory of Nyssa (355–398), Giordano Bruno (1548–1600), and Emanuel Swedenborg (1688–1772), just to name a few. Although they did not use the scientific language to explain a multidimensional universe, they nevertheless described it and knew it existed. Had modern science accepted these "fairy tales" decades ago as the visions of people who had the ability to see beyond the physical universe rather than the pipe dreams of those trying to escape reality, we might have a better understanding of the human condition today.

TEN

THE CURRENT SITUATION

Recently I was invited to a gathering of people in Greenwich, Connecticut, which was hosted by well-known psychic Joan Carra. Joan is one of those rare individuals who have the ability to see into these other realms of existence. She has a keen insight and is truly a citizen of many worlds. Joan has had a number of UFO-related experiences as well as contact with beings that could be angelic in nature. Inspired by these contacts, Joan has composed several beautiful poems, which have been set to music. These poems relate a number of her experiences, which for the most part seem to be all positive in nature. Joan's psychic ability has been documented in the media and her actual contact with extra- or ultraterrestrial beings seems to be on the psychic level. Joan refers to these contact experiences as "dreams," but she knows they are actual communications with a higher intelligence. Although she has had a multitude of experiences, I will present one here in her own words.

"In this 'dream,' I was sittings at the control board of a spaceship with very tall Nordic-looking humans teaching me how to use it. These fair-skinned, blonde people were as tall as, if not taller than, basketball players—well over seven feet. I used to be a board operator at a public radio station, and also took a class in audio engineering, so I was comfortable manning the controls of the spaceship. It had a familiarity to it and that was the reason why they were showing me how to use it. The extraterrestrials' explanation of space travel was so fascinating that when it was time for the dream to end, I didn't want to wake up. I wanted to stay with my visitors and learn more.

"All day, I was longing to go back to the dream. I knew it had valuable information that was now lost to wake-up's amnesia. I decided to meditate and try to access the information from my subconscious mind. I closed my eyes and slowed down my breathing. Then it happened—I saw in my mind's eye a diagram of a cylinder with a different galaxy on the top and bottom of it. The cylinder then shrank and the top and bottom planes met. The ovals also spun to align the galaxy on point A on the top and galaxy on point B on the bottom. The cylinder was now one oval with one point, which was both galaxy A and B."

The information contained in this dream was interesting because to me it sounded like advanced string theory, and in this case, space was not warped or folded for space travel (as in *Star Trek*), but compressed at two points in the physical universe. This idea is quite advanced, and if true, spacefaring beings could traverse the entire universe in minutes or weeks rather than thousands or millions of years.

There were also a number of other people at this gathering who had had a past paranormal or UFO experience. I feel it is very important for people who have had these encounters to get together once in a while to share their stories and compare notes. It is my belief that many people who are involved in a spiritual quest are somehow geared into that direction with a past extraterrestrial contact or paranormal experience providing the driving force.

During the course of the afternoon, there were many stories of UFO sightings and encounters, which to me sounded like some level of contact with interdimensional entities. One individual who quickly caught my interest was an ex-Buddhist monk by the name of Greg who, without a doubt, seemed to be connected to a higher intelligence. Greg had constructed a number of devices that channel energy for healing and meditation. They consisted of what looked like Lucite glass or lead crystal cut into hexagonal geometric patterns. Attached to the Lucite were copper coils in a number of interesting forms wound tightly at the top and bottom of the object. I was surprised to see that the "instruments" had a striking resemblance to some of the devices channeled through Mr. Dean Fagerstrom (Dean's case appears in my book, *Contact of the 5th Kind*) from the angelic entity Donestra.

I was not really sure how Greg got the idea to build these things, but from what I heard from the conversation that day, they could have been the result of some type of contact experience. What the extent of this contact was I never found out, since I had to leave before I could question him in greater detail. All in all, it was a very nice afternoon talking with intelligent people who, like me, are searching for answers.

It's amazing that there are so many people out there that have had UFO sightings and some type of contact with an alien or interdimensional intelligence. On July 26, 2007, I spoke at the Staatsburg Library in Staatsburg, New York, a small town in the northern Hudson Valley on the east side of the river. After my PowerPoint presentation of the UFO experience, a number of people approached me to relate sightings of the Hudson Valley UFO that they had had all the way back in 1984! It has been my experience from questions asked during my lectures that only 2 percent of all the people who had a UFO sighting talk about it; the rest stay silent. Some may wait a very long time after their sighting to tell someone because they feel safer to talk about it after many years have passed. To me, this 2 percent represents thousands, and the actual number of individuals worldwide must be staggering—it is truly a hidden epidemic. Can all of these people be nothing more than psychotics or dreamers trying to escape the reality of a cruel, harsh world by inventing a fantasy to escape to? I think not.

UFO OVER NEW YORK CITY

During the great UFO wave from 1983 to 1990 over most of southern New York, I was often asked why there were few reports from New York City, where there are thousands of possible witnesses at any given time. The majority of people in the city of New York go about their business in quite a hurry, not paying attention to anything else. This is why when a UFO was visible in the sky during the day or night, very few people actually looked up, and when they did, most of these people didn't care what they saw as long as the tops of the buildings weren't falling down to the ground. The following report of a sighting back in the late winter of 1986 was recently sent to me. The witness's name is Rosebud (yes, real name), and she was leaving a movie on Eighth Street. Her report clearly supports my idea about why NYC residents do not see or report UFO encounters. The following is the account of Rosebud's sighting in her own words.

"The movie let out at 9:30 p.m. When we hit the street, my husband and I realized that the temperature had plummeted and it was wickedly cold. We set off briskly for East Twelfth Street, talking about the movie and the cold and getting home where it was warm. We'd kept our heads lowered turtle-like in our scarves, scuttling along like everyone else on the street. The night was glorious, the sky was black and clear. We stopped for the light on Eighth Street and Lafayette, looking both ways for traffic. My husband saw it first. I tugged on his elbow to move, but he stopped. He was staring down Lafayette Street, fascinated. 'What's that?' he asked, pointing south. 'How odd. Look at those planes.' In the distance, below Houston Street, there was indeed what appeared to be a perfect formation of brightly lit airplanes, nine of them in a V formation like a flock of geese, but they were flying much too slowly and much too low.

"Now we were both fixed. They were still approaching, the golden lights, slow and unwavering. 'I don't think these are planes,' I ventured to say. We stood there on the freezing corner, pulling closer together, discussing just what it might be. Because it seemed quite certain now that it was

not a formation, it was singular. The lights were too perfectly spaced; it was all too harmonious with no sound.

"Any sort of common flying machine makes noise. If you
spot a light plane, or helicopter, or jet, even a mile or more
above, you can always hear their thin, distinctive sound. What
was approaching now was sailing grandly along, barely clearing the tops of the low buildings, no more than eight stories
above the street, without a whisper. My husband now was in
doubt about planes. It was still approaching, steady on, and
I'd forgotten the cold. Now it was close enough to see that
it was indeed all one piece—the lights forming a sort of boomerang, the leading sides of something gigantic and triangular. It floated silently as the moon, so unhurried, so leisurely
that a person could jog along quickly and keep pace with it.
Only two streets away now, and I began to feel fear. It was
sailing slowly, gloriously on, past the Public Theater. 'You
know what that is,' I urged, wanting my husband to verify, to
reassure, to collaborate. But 'No, I don't,' he said. I began to
glance around to see who else was gazing up into the sky, but
no one was.

"There must have been a hundred people darting back and
forth around Astor Place, but the cold was propelling them.
Everyone was looking down, scuttling like spiders, hurry-
ing along to escape the bite of the cold. I desperately needed
someone else to see what we were seeing. Two nattily dressed
young Spanish guys halted beside us at the light. I plucked at
one's sleeve. 'Please,' I said, pointing. 'What is that?' 'Whoa!
A UFO! Check it out!' They laughed delightedly, bent over
at the waist, slapped each others hands, and kept walking. I

couldn't believe it! They crossed the street, looking up at it occasionally, pointing and laughing. 'Am I insane? Are they high? What's going on here?' In desperation, I called out to another very straight-looking couple turning the corner. I pointed. 'Oh!' said the girl. 'Oh, my God!' Her boyfriend was blasé at first—big deal, a plane. But then he realized that this was not, in fact, a plane, or a helicopter. Or even a blimp, which anyway wouldn't have clearance to fly at night, almost grazing buildings! She told us that this was what she'd seen the year before, in France, but never so close. Her boyfriend seemed to want to get away from it then, so he pulled her firmly off down the street. They both turned their heads a few times to look back, looking bewildered.

"By now it was cruising majestically onto Astor Place. It was no more than eighty feet above us. The black clarity of the night revealed every pinpoint star, but as this monumental thing sailed directly overhead, except for the lights along its edge, it blotted out the sky. It seemed to absorb or muffle all sound, or more likely I was so focused on it that everything else fell away, the cold, and the sounds of the street. It sailed over the parking lot, and the beloved sculpture of the Cube that stood on its small concrete island in the intersection. You can estimate the size of things above by holding your arms out straight above you at an object and measuring from fingertip to fingertip. Factoring in the approximate height of it, I realized that it was at least two-hundred feet long. It was, indeed, nearly as big as a football field!

"My voice failed me, and my common sense. I didn't call out to anyone else, although dozens of people were crossing back and forth along the avenue. I clutched at my husband, and with my free arm I hugged the lamppost tightly. *I am looking up at this*, I thought. *And it, presumably, is looking down at me.* I ached with awe, and fear, and love for this mystery. I wanted to reach my hand up, and stroke the sleek blackness of its underbelly, but I thought that if ever I could, I would be sucked away into some infinity for which I was yet unprepared. As it glided soundlessly north, still just above the rooftops, I felt myself shivering with relief. We watched it lift slightly, light as a bubble, and head away, out of our vision in the direction of Union Square. I realized that my eyes were full of tears, I think from the cold.

"I've never forgotten it. The incident is still as clear in my mind as it was that night. It convinced me, once and for all, that we are visited by beings from other worlds. I read the books and watch the UFO programs even more avidly, hoping to learn more about what I saw. And every time I cross Astor Place, I lightly run my fingers along the lamppost that I clutched that night and remember my awe. I glance down Lafayette Street and remember . . . I still think, *If such a thing was floating by at nine thirty on a busy night, what is hovering over the deserted streets at five o'clock in the morning?*"

There is no doubt that Rosebud and her husband saw the Hudson Valley UFO that night. Perhaps when this account is published, more people who saw the object in NYC that night will come forward with their own sighting reports.

A CONTACT ENCOUNTER ON A LAKE

In some cases, people are physically abducted and they experience what has been referred to in UFO research as "missing time." These people only remember seeing the UFO, but they almost never recall seeing the object leave. They also notice that several hours have passed after a sighting, which they thought was only fifteen minutes or less. In some of these cases, an onboard experience and contact with a non-human intelligence is revealed under hypnosis, but sometimes there is just a blank in their memory. Perhaps when certain people are taken, they are kept unconscious and have no recollection of the "onboard" experience.

The following report was made to me in 2007 by a person who had a close encounter in 1984 when he was nineteen years old. I found this case interesting because it took place in the Hudson Valley on the same night that a great number of sightings were taking place over Putnam, Westchester, and Dutchess counties. The witness, whose real first name is Andy, related his account on Lake Whaley in Holmes, New York (Dutchess County), sometime during the last week of July 1984.

"This event happened right after one of the UFO sightings (July 24) at the Indian Point nuclear reactor facility, which is located about thirty miles southwest of our location. My best friend and I decided to go out to look at the stars, as it was clear that night. So at dusk, about eight thirty or so, we got in a small rowboat powered by an electric motor and set out across the lake towards the train tracks.

"There was a great deal of activity in the sky, such as heat lightning, planes, and what sounded like the end of a fireworks show far off in the distance. After about a twenty-minute ride in the boat, we looked in the opposite direction of the sky, and I saw a searchlight scanning the railroad tracks on the south-middle side of the lake. I heard no sound, so it could not have been a helicopter or plane. We freaked out and then it vanished.

"I can estimate that the distance from our boat to the railroad tracks where we saw the searchlight was less than two hundred feet. I remember it as a white light, and as it was shining down, it was moving as if it was searching the tracks. I remember looking up to the sky and wondering where the hell it was coming from.

"We then headed north where there are no houses for about a half-mile and then saw an incredible bright fluttering light that was about fifteen to twenty feet above the tracks and heading out of the woods. My immediate thought was *it's a train*, which quickly turned to fear as it stopped at the edge of the tracks and the water, and again not a sound at all!

"So my best friend and I turned off the putt-putt boat motor and were wondering what the hell it was, and by now we were very scared. After watching the light for a short time, we turned the motor on and began to move toward the light. As soon as we began to move, the light came directly towards us, and before it met us, we turned the boat around and retreated, and the light did the same.

"Now let me try to describe the light. It was the brightest thing I have ever seen and although it was stationary, it was fluttering with the colors of white, amber, and green. I recall more of a fireball than an object. We again headed towards the light and it again headed to us. We chickened out again and turned around and the light did the same. At last we said, 'Let's go for it and see what happens.' This time we met the light somewhere in the middle.

"The light went around the boat, and I could not see it and asked my friend where it was. At this time he was illuminated by a light and I could feel heat on the back of my shoulder, and my friend cried out that the light was behind me. I estimated that it was about fifteen feet from the boat and the same height above the water. I asked my friend what the light felt like, which was still on him, and he replied almost in tears that it felt like every molecule in his body was being vibrated. We were terrified, and I would say from the time we saw the light flying down from the train tracks until it disappeared was fifteen to twenty minutes, but I don't remember the light leaving. Another thing, when we got home, it was around midnight. We left around eight thirty and the entire boat ride was about ninety minutes long (two hours of unaccounted time).

"I am forty-one years old and own and operate a small masonry business. I had lost track of my friend since 1989, but I did locate him in the fall of 2006, and after not talking to him for seventeen years and after he answered the phone within fifteen minutes we were talking about the sighting. We both witnessed the exact same thing and never reported it to any authorities, and if I had been alone, I would be convinced that I was insane.

"I have always considered getting hypnotized to try to bring out more detail, but never have. I have always tried to convince myself that the timeline was off and no missing time exists, but my friend, who recalled more vivid details and exact times, is positive we were not out that long."

It could be that during the possible missing two hours, Andy and his friend were scanned, studied, and then perhaps rejected by this intelligence. It's too bad that Andy waited this long to report his sighting, since the incident could have been properly investigated when the trail was still hot. Recently, I have been getting e-mail at a rate of several messages a week from people who had UFO sightings as far back as 1957! It could be that UFOs are being accepted more in our society and, although still cautious, most witnesses no longer fear ridicule.

THE EXPERIENCES OF HAROLD EGELN JR

The first time that I met Harold was at a UFO conference in Manhattan during the mid-to-late eighties. As soon as he introduced himself to me, I knew that he had a deep connection to the UFO phenomenon, much more than an interest. He had told me of an experience that he had on Reservoir and Upper Magnetic mine roads in Brewster, New York. I was a little taken aback at the time because I had already received a number of reports from the exact area of alien encounters on the road close to one of the stone chambers. Harold was drawn to Brewster because of the recent accounts of UFO activity in the Hudson Valley and on August 11, 1988, he and a friend decided to visit the area.

They made arrangements to stay overnight on August 12 and 13 at a home in Westchester County, New York, and on the night of August 12, they went out to explore the countryside. Harold was drawn to a lonely dirt road called Reservoir in the town of Southeast (South Brewster). As they got out of the car and walked around, Harold became frightened and uncomfortable, so they left and returned to the house. I found this statement interesting since they were in the exact location of a very strong magnetic anomaly, one so strong that it was studied in great detail by the last Geophysical Year. People whom I have brought out to this area feel uneasy and the effect seems to last for several days. Also, as mentioned earlier, there is no coincidence that a stone chamber (see chapter five) is located forty-three feet from this magnetic disturbance. There is no way that Harold could have known about the anomaly, and I have found that people who are very sensitive or have psychic abilities appear to be more affected by it.

On August 14, 1988, they returned to the same area on Reservoir Road. Harold's friend did a meditation, while he slowly walked away from her. Looking toward the reservoir, he noticed what looked like large, glowing, slanted green eyes and large, hairless heads floating through the woods many yards out from the road; there seemed to be five in all. He called out to his friend, who also saw them, and when he did this, the "heads and eyes" stopped moving. As if responding to the creatures in the woods, a large dog started barking and was getting closer to their location, so they got concerned and jumped in their rented car.

During the night of May 26–27, 1991, Harold returned to Reservoir Road in Brewster with a group of people. As soon as they arrived, they heard a pinging sound, and shortly after that, three or four of the people with him felt a tingling or electric-like feeling in their hands. They then noticed a shaft of subtle white light on the road, and as Harold walked into the circle, he reported to the others that it was very cold. Although the temperature that night was in the seventies, the area within the faint circle of light was, as Harold reported, "freezing."

After a very short time, they saw a white outline appear on the road about fifty feet in front of them. It was in the shape of a saucer with a dome on top. The light then faded and they saw figures, which looked like they were in hooded robes, scurrying across the road. As Harold moved down the road, a scream came from the car where two others of his party were sitting. The person in the car (whom Harold called Cherry) claimed to have seen three little gray beings moving toward the back of the car, only to disappear when she screamed. Harold then continued to walk down the road to get a better view of the hooded beings. He could barely see them on the side, and as a car came down the road, the beings seemed to bow or duck down as if they didn't want to be seen. Harold and the others then noticed the hooded beings walk into the large outcropping of rock along the side of the road, where they vanished. After they passed through the rock, in front of it there appeared a swirling vortex that looked like a hurricane.

Amazed at what they saw, they talked about what just happened and then after ten minutes the shadowy hooded beings emerged from the rock and settled right across the road from Harold and another member of his party. Harold felt compelled to approach them, but his friend stayed back. As Harold got closer, he felt a "wall of positive and negative emotions" sweep through him. Harold could no longer see the beings, but his friend and the others who were still down the road could still see their outlines. As the others watched, they noticed that the hooded beings were now surrounding Harold. The others tried calling out to him to let him know that the creatures were all around him, but Harold saw nothing.

Harold then felt energy throughout his entire body and up his spine as if experiencing G-force acceleration. Then the experience ended and the mysterious entities were gone.

For a month afterward, Harold felt like his heart was wide open and filled with happiness. One could easily dismiss this case as the product of mass hysteria and the work of a number of overactive imaginations working together to create the illusion of extraterrestrial contact. However, I believe that the encounter that Harold had with his companions was a real event. During this time, Harold seemed to have had some type of communication or contact with beings that appear to have been interdimensional in nature. A short time later, Harold founded the New York City–based organization SPACE, which is dedicated to the research and exploration of contact with interdimensional and extraterrestrial beings. The hooded beings of Reservoir Road have been spotted many times since 1899, and sightings are still being reported.

In my files I have 342 contact cases. The cases, I feel, are real, and the people involved are stable individuals whose lives were turned upside down because of the experience. I was able to divide the cases into two categories, the first involving extraterrestrials and the second, interdimensional and psychic contacts. I tried to find a common thread to the cases, and this is what I discovered:

1. All the individuals in the second category demonstrated active or dormant psychic ability compared to only 27 percent in the first category.

2. Of all the people in the second category, 92 percent had an encounter or a so-called imaginary friend as a child.

3. Of the 342 cases, 72 percent indicate extraterrestrial contacts involving the "grays" and the classical abduction scenario; 72 percent were female, while 28 percent were male; the peak age of both sexes was fifteen to forty-three; and 83 percent of the females had B negative blood type, while the blood type of the males varied.

4. Of the 342 cases, 28 percent involved interdimensional contacts, such as angels, jinn, and channeling, with male and female reports divided almost equally. The peak age for both sexes was thirty-five to sixty.

The majority of these contacts took place at night and most had an individual history of UFO encounters while a smaller number had no UFO sightings at all. In a large number of these cases in which encounters took place in the person's bedroom, "sleep paralysis" was reported. (This is the feeling of being unable to move while conscious in bed during the night.) It is my belief that the phenomenon known as sleep paralysis is not easily explainable in the conventional sense. Many psychologists believe that you are really dreaming when you think you are awake, and that is why you can't move. The people proposing this theory don't even consider the paranormal aspect, and once again events like this are being explained away by "experts" who have never experienced it for themselves.

I am convinced that sleep paralysis is a prelude to the contact experience. The beings who make contact, whether angels, jinn, or extraterrestrials, may be trying to communicate and, to stop the person from jumping out of bed, they neutralize the electrical impulses going from the brain to the muscles. It is at this time that gentle or aggressive contact can be made. Many people who have experienced this have a sense of dread, and when they begin to hear voices, they focus their energy to try to snap out of it. Some concentrate on the white light from the soul or even call upon God or Jesus for help. Or, they just plain get angry and use aggressive energy to break the hold. All those who have experienced this physical phenomenon report that it feels very ominous—some even feel violated.

I have experienced sleep paralysis on a number of occasions, and it is not a pleasant thing. During this time I have not seen anything but have felt a presence in the room with me and actually felt something trying to hold on to me. On a number of occasions I have heard voices; sometimes I could understand what they were saying, but other times it was some unknown language.

Over the years I have found that the investigation and research of UFOs and paranormal phenomena was more of a spiritual journey and learning experience for me than a scientific research project, as it was originally meant to be those many years ago. To all my readers out there who are experienced paranormal investigators and to those just starting out, the advice I give to you is to remember that *all of this is very real!* If you plan to get involved, then I suggest you seek the counsel of those who have been out there for some time. Also, seek the advice of a reputable proven psychic to act as a counselor and guide as you journey into the unknown. You will be taking a large step into a new world, and you're going to need all the help you can get to keep your wits. The human race is like a child at the beach, ankle deep in the water, looking out to the ocean. The water feels good to us and we would like to walk out farther, but we must be cautious, because the cosmic ocean is vast and filled with many mysteries and dangers.

Good journey on your quest.

IMPORTANT UFO EVENTS IN THE TWENTIETH CENTURY

1945: Horten aircraft documents discovered by the American Army in Germany

1947: Ken Arnold sighting
Roswell "crash"
Project MOGUL begins
Project Sign/Saucer begins

1949: Project Grudge begins

1951: Project Blue Book begins

1952: the first civilian organizations form to investigate UFOs

1953: FBI begins paranormal investigations

1959: William Booth Gill sighting

1961: Barney and Betty Hill "alien abduction"

1965: Exeter, New Hampshire, sightings
Astronauts White and McDivitt report UFO in space

1969: Air Force announces end of UFO study and closes
project Blue Book

1975: author begins investigating UFOs

1983: Hudson Valley UFO sightings

1987: Gulf Breeze UFO sightings

1990: Belgium UFO sightings

1997: Paulden, Arizona, UFO sightings

LISTING OF INDIVIDUALS AND ORGANIZATIONS YOU MAY WANT TO CONTACT FOR FURTHER INFORMATION

Philip Imbrogno
c/o Llewellyn Worldwide, Ltd.
2143 Wooddale Drive, Dept. 978-0-7387-1347-2
Woodbury, MN 55125-2989
E-mail: Bel1313@yahoo.com

Joan Carra *(psychic)*
c/o TRS Professional Suite
44 East 32nd St.
New York, NY 10016

Loretta Chaney *(psychic)*
Website: www.lorettachaney.net
E-mail: info@lorettachaney.net

Posey Gilbert *(researcher)*
110 Rockaway Parkway #2
Brooklyn, NY 11212
Website: templeoftheinfidel.com
E-mail: bplgeus@optonline.net

Reverend Michael Carter *(researcher)*
E-mail: mjcarter9@msn.com

Tami Haines *(paranormal investigator)*
E-mail: hainest@dejazzed.com

The Mutual UFO Network *(civilian UFO research group)*
PO Box 369
Morrison, CO 80465-0369

The Center for UFO Studies *(civilian UFO research group)*
2457 W Peterson Ave
Chicago, IL 60659

New England Antiquities Association
Contact: Betty Peterson
1199 Main Street
Worcester, MA 01603

Open membership provides research into stone chambers and
other megalithic sites in New England and New York.

Search Project for Aspects of Close Encounters (SPACE)

Web page: http://community-2.webtv.net/HEgeln/SPACE
SearchProject/

UFO Magazine

PO Box 11013

Marina del Rey, CA 90295

An excellent publication that covers UFOs and related phenomena.

BIBLIOGRAPHY
AND CITATIONS

Although most of the material used in this book comes from my own investigation files, the following resources were used to supplement the information. The listing of this material can also be used as suggestions for outstanding books to further your interest in the subject matter. Except for my own books, public documents, and information that was handed down to me by some of the late, great UFO researchers, all supplemental material was analyzed and interpreted to fill some of the few gaps in my research.

MY CASE FILES

The majority of information and data in this book was taken from my case files. Over the past thirty years, I have collected detailed reports of the most complex paranormal events with detailed investigation and scientific findings with complete laboratory reports and analysis of video, film, digital images, and computer databases.

BOOKS AND PUBLICATIONS

Abbott, Edwin. *Flatland: A Romance of Many Dimensions*. Mineola, NY: Dover, 1992.

Casteel, Sean, and Timothy Green Beckley. *Our Alien Planet: This Eerie Earth*. New Brunswick, NJ: Inner Light/Global Communications, 2005.

Constable, Trevor J. *The Cosmic Pulse of Life: The Revolutionary Biological Power Behind UFOs*. Eureka, CA: Borderland Sciences, 1990.

Fawcett, Lawrence, and Barry J. Greenwood. *Clear Intent: The Government Coverup of the UFO Experience*. Englewood Cliffs, NJ: Prentice Hall, 1984.

Fuller, John G. *The Incident at Exeter: Unidentified Flying Objects Over America Now*. New York, NY: G.P. Putnam's Sons, 1967.

Fuller, John G. *The Interrupted Journey Two Lost Hours "Aboard a Flying Saucer."* London: Souvenir Press, Ltd., 1970.

Hynek, J. Allen. *The UFO Experience: A Scientific Inquiry*. New York, NY: Marlowe Publishing, 1998.

Hynek, J. Allen, Philip J. Imbrogno, and Bob Pratt. *Night Siege: The Hudson Valley UFO Sightings*. 2nd ed. St. Paul, MN: Llewellyn, 1998.

Imbrogno, Philip. *Crosswalks Across the Universe: A Guide to Amateur Astronomy*. New York, NY: Vantage Press, 1980.

Imbrogno, Philip J. "Imaging Satellites in Space Using Your PC." *Earth Magazine*, May 1992.

Imbrogno, Philip J. *UFO Universe*. Articles from 1983–89.

Imbrogno, Philip J., and Marianne Horrigan. *Contact of the 5th Kind*. St. Paul, MN: Llewellyn, 1997.

Imbrogno, Philip J., and Marianne Horrigan. *Celtic Mysteries in New England*. St. Paul, MN: Llewellyn Publishing, 2000.

Imbrogno, Philip J., and Marianne Horrigan. *Celtic Mysteries: Windows to Another Dimension in America's Northeast*. New York, NY: Cosimo/Paraview Publishing, 2005.

Keel, John. *Operation Trojan Horse*. Lilburn, GA: IllumiNet Press, 1996.

Morison, Samuel Eliot. *Admiral of the Ocean Sea: A Life of Christopher Columbus*. New York, NY: Time Inc., 1962.

Sanderson, Ivan T. *Uninvited Visitors: A Biologist Looks at UFOs*. New York, NY: Cowles Education Corporation, 1967.

DOCUMENTS

Documents were obtained using the Freedom of Information Act and a visit to the National Archives before it became almost impossible to use due to the so-called Patriot Act. The following documents were examined or copies obtained at the National Archives.

A History of the Sargasso Sea. United States Coast Guard Document H11758, September 1964.

The Horten Wing. Air Material Command, 1947. Declassified 1955.

Investigation of Anomalies Phenomena. Federal Bureau of Investigation case files from 1950–67. Declassified August 1982.

Project Blue Book. United States Air Force, 1970.

Project MOGUL. Army Air Corps document, declassified 1999.

Project Saucer/Sign Conclusions. Air Material Command, 1951.

Project Twinkle. Air Material Command, 1951.

The Roswell Case Closed. United States Air Force, 1997 document.

United States Coast Guard Report, file number LIS12-03-72: *Analysis of USO* (underwater submarine activity in Long Island Sound, New York).

United States Navy Report #345643AB, involving disappearances of ships and electrical phenomena off the coast of Bermuda. Declassified 1986.

Files were obtained from the United States Air Force after a lengthy conversation with them in 1987. Over twenty-five files were sent to me concerning UFO reports in the Hudson Valley, New York, by the Federal Aviation Administration. These files include numbers AF-20.536, AFD-8103, and AFD-200.6, plus a copy of a personal letter to researcher and co-author of *Night Siege* Bob Pratt that he had never received.

SOURCES OF OTHER DOCUMENTATION

Some material is based on raw case information given to me for my research and mutual projects in publication or the electronic media by the late UFO researchers John Burton, John G. Fuller, Ron Simjian, Dr. J. Allen Hynek, and finally Bob Pratt, after their passing.

INDEX

Free Catalog

Get the latest
information on our
body, mind, and spirit products!
To receive a **free** copy of Llewellyn's consumer
magazine, *New Worlds of Mind & Spirit,* simply
call 1-877-NEW-WRLD or visit our website at
www.llewellyn.com and click on *New Worlds.*

🌙 LLEWELLYN ORDERING INFORMATION

Order Online:
Visit our website at www.llewellyn.com, select your books, and order
them on our secure server.

Order by Phone:
- Call toll-free within the U.S. at 1-877-NEW-WRLD
  (1-877-639-9753). Call toll-free within Canada at
  1-866-NEW-WRLD (1-866-639-9753)
- We accept VISA, MasterCard, and American Express

Order by Mail:
Send the full price of your order (MN residents add 6.5% sales tax) in
U.S. funds, plus postage & handling to:

> **Llewellyn Worldwide**
> **2143 Wooddale Drive, Dept. 978-0-7387-1347-2**
> **Woodbury, MN 55125-2989, U.S.A.**

Postage & Handling:

> **Standard** (U.S., Mexico, & Canada). If your order is:
> > $24.99 and under, add $3.00
> > $25.00 and over, FREE STANDARD SHIPPING
>
> AK, HI, PR: $15.00 for one book plus $1.00 for
> each additional book.
>
> **International Orders** (airmail only):
> > $16.00 for one book plus $3.00 for each additional book

Orders are processed within 2 business days.
Please allow for normal shipping time. Postage and handling rates subject to change.

Night Siege
The Hudson Valley UFO Sightings

DR. J. ALLEN HYNEK,
PHILIP J. IMBROGNO, & BOB PRATT

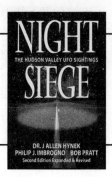

Since 1983, more than seven thousand people have reported seeing a large UFO above New York's Hudson Valley. But the media keeps silent about it, as do the military and the FAA. Now, top UFO investigators reveal evidence that cannot be denied. A classic in the field, *Night Siege* has been called one of the best-researched UFO books to date.

978-1-56718-362-7
288 pp., 5¼ x 8 $9.95

UFOs Over Topanga Canyon
Eyewitness Accounts of the
California Sightings

PRESTON DENNETT

The rural Californian community of Topanga Canyon is home
to eight thousand close-knit residents, the Topanga State Park,
and an unusual amount of strange activity going on in the sky.

Like Hudson Valley, NY, and Gulf Breeze, FL, Topanga Canyon is considered a UFO hotspot, with sightings that began
more than fifty years ago and continue to this day. Here is the
first book to present the activity in the witnesses' own words.

Read new cases of unexplained lights, metallic ships, beams
of light, face-to-face alien encounters, UFO healings, strange
animal sightings, animal mutilations, and evidence of a government cover-up. There are even six cases involving missing
time abductions, and a possible onboard UFO experience.

978-1-56718-221-7
312 pp., 5 ³/₁₆ x 8 $12.95

To order, call 1-877-NEW-WRLD
Prices subject to change without notice

The Fog

A Never Before Published Theory of the Bermuda Triange Phenomenon

ROB MACGREGOR & BRUCE GERNON

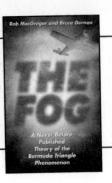

Is there an explanation for the thousands of people who have disappeared in the Bermuda Triangle? What can we learn from Charles Lindbergh, Christopher Columbus, and Bruce Gernon—the coauthor of this book—who have survived their frightening encounters in this region?

The Fog presents Gernon's exciting new theory of the Bermuda Triangle, based upon his firsthand experiences, reports of other survivors, and scientific research. Gernon and MacGregor intelligently discuss how a meteorological phenomenon—electronic fog—may explain the bizarre occurrences in this region: equipment malfunctions, disorientation among pilots, and time distortions. They also explore the fascinating history of this infamous region and its potential link to Atlantis, UFO sightings, and a secret navy base on Andros Island.

978-0-7387-0757-0
240 pp., 5 ³/₁₆ x 8   **$12.95**

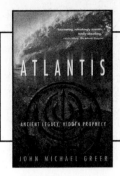

Atlantis
Ancient Legacy, Hidden Prophecy

JOHN MICHAEL GREER

Is there anything our modern industrial society can learn from the story of Atlantis, a legend that has endured for two thousand years?

From the dialogues of Plato to the modern age of Atlantology, esteemed occultist John Michael Greer traces the evolution of this controversial story about a great civilization drowned by the sea. See how this fascinating legend was reshaped by modern occultists and pioneers of the "rejected knowledge" movement. Greer also proposes his own revolutionary theory—based on Plato's accounts, human history, and geological science—of a civilization doomed by natural disasters at the end of the last Ice Age.

As the threat of global warming makes headlines today, Greer poses the ultimate question: is the legend of Atlantis a legacy of the distant past, or a prophecy of our own future?

978-0-7387-0978-9
264 pp., 6 x 9, hardcover $21.95

TO WRITE TO THE AUTHOR

If you wish to contact the author or would like more information about this book, please write to the author in care of Llewellyn Worldwide and we will forward your request. Both the author and publisher appreciate hearing from you and learning of your enjoyment of this book and how it has helped you. Llewellyn Worldwide cannot guarantee that every letter written to the author can be answered, but all will be forwarded. Please write to:

Philip Imbrogno
c/o Llewellyn Worldwide
2143 Wooddale Drive, Dept. 978-0-7387-1347-2
Woodbury, MN 55125-2989, U.S.A.

Please enclose a self-addressed stamped envelope for reply,
or $1.00 to cover costs. If outside U.S.A., enclose
international postal reply coupon.

Many of Llewellyn's authors have websites with additional information and resources. For more information, please visit our website at:

www.llewellyn.com